YOU
ONLY
DIE
ONCE

YOU ONLY DIE ONCE

PREPARING FOR THE END OF LIFE
WITH **GRACE** AND **GUSTO**

MARGIE JENKINS

INTEGRITY®
PUBLISHERS
Nashville

You Only Die Once

HELPING PEOPLE WORLDWIDE EXPERIENCE *the* MANIFEST PRESENCE *of* GOD.

Published in association with Balcony Author Services,
P.O. Box 92, Salado, Texas 76571.

Because of the sensitive nature of the personal stories in this book, some of the names have been changed.

Scriptures quoted are from The Holy Bible, New International Version, copyright © 1973, 1978, 1984, International Bible Society. Used by permission of Zondervan Bible Publishers.

More information on Margie Jenkins is available on her Web Site:
www.margiejenkins.com

Library of Congress Cataloging-in-Publication Data

Jenkins, Margie Little.
   You only die once: planning for the end of life with grace and gusto / Margie
Little Jenkins.
   ISBN 1-59145-013-6
   1. Death—Planning.   2. Death—United States—Planning.   3. Death—
Social aspects—United States.   4. Death—Psychological aspects.
5. Bereavement—Psychological aspects.   I. Title: planning for the end of life
with grace and gusto.   II. Title.
HQ1073.J45   2002
306.9–dc21
                                                                    2002068525

Printed in the United States of America
02 03 04 05 06 07 08 09 BP 9 8 7 6 5 4 3 2 1

To Jenks,

my husband of fifty-six years,

my editor, my best friend, my lover,

who encouraged me through every page

of this book.

Disclaimer: The personal experiences in *You Only Die Once* are true. Names and other identifying details have been changed to protect the privacy of those involved. If incidents described in this book seem familiar to the reader, it is because these experiences occur frequently and, although often not understood at the time, gain clarity in retrospect.

CONTENTS

Acknowledgments

Jenks, my husband and resident editor, read every word, offered ideas, and made me laugh. Without Francis Heatherley of Balcony Author Services, this book would never have happened. His tireless support and belief in the subject provided me courage and determination to keep plowing on even when I thought I had gone as far as I could go. Ramona Richards, the publisher's editor, had faith in me and the goals of this book. Dr. Charlie W. Shedd mentored me for more than fifty years. Our daughters, Susan Suberbielle and Toby Howard Gilbert, and their husbands, Tom and Joe, were willing to discuss this book endlessly. Our sons, Rick and Bob, and their wives, Dede and Nancy, cheered me on. My special friend Claire Ashley inspired me to revise what I thought was already finished and made me more proud of the result. And my good friend Franz Ehrhardt suggested the title for the book. My clients shared their lives and stories with me. My parents, Mom and Dad Little, gave me their best. I know they are in heaven applauding my efforts. To all of you who have shared an interest and reassurance, I thank you for your love.

Introduction

The other day I saw a bumper sticker that read "Life is hell, and then you die." (Okay, so I cleaned it up a little.) And I thought, "It really doesn't have to be that way."

I am convinced that everyone can live "bodaciously." Of course, no one can sift all the pain out of life, but by looking and planning ahead instead of allowing life to just happen helter-skelter, you can experience more pleasure and fulfillment during your earthly journey.

This is especially true of the last chapter of life. To be sure, you don't know everything that's going to happen in your final days. So on the basis of meager knowledge of the future, you can make excuses for not preparing for it. You can leave everything from unwritten wills to nonexistent burial arrangements to plop down into the laps of your loved ones two seconds after you breathe your last breath. In the meantime, you live with all that unfinished business uncomfortably hanging over your head.

How would you like to be free of that nagging back-of-your-mind baggage for the rest of your days and nights? What if you had the peace of mind that comes with knowing that, immediately after your death, your children and other loved ones will not have to worry about what kind of funeral you want and whether you prefer to be buried or cremated? Or wonder where your insurance policies are filed, or how their inheritance will be passed down, and a dozen other things like that? Wouldn't that in itself add a great measure of zest to your life?

Looking back, I now realize that the genesis for this book was evident throughout my entire life. Years ago, when it was time for me to choose a course of study in college, I wanted to help people get more fun out of life. At Girl Scout camp, the counselors seemed to have the best time, I thought, so maybe camp counseling would be the right major for me. But such a degree did not rank high on the list for my college-educated parents. They were community minded and traditional in thinking that their offspring should make more of a difference in the world. So I majored in health education.

After getting married, teaching at William Woods College in Fulton, Missouri, raising four kids, and being active in a local Presbyterian church, I decided, at age fifty, to get a master's degree at the University of Houston and write a column for my hometown paper, *The Kentucky Post*. I found a new passion when I became a human relations consultant and a psychotherapist for individuals, couples, families, and groups. My clients share their lives and stories with me when they are distressed, frustrated, facing broken dreams, or just looking for more positive directions. They come seeking hope and guidance to make their lives more satisfying and significant. My lifework embraces love and meaning, which is the theme of this book.

One segment of my work focuses on cancer patients and their families, and helping them find more happiness, understanding, and peace. Planning for life's final chapter is a common subject in my office, along with aiding survivors in creating a new life.

Using the experience I've gained, I began leading workshops on various subjects, such as effective communication, developing coping skills, retirement planning, and caring for aging parents. When B. J. Frye, a leader in our church and my friend for thirty years, called in May 1997, she urged me to repeat a successful seminar called Writing Your Own Story. Instead, I suggested we come up with a fresh idea.

B. J. had been receiving chemotherapy treatments for several months, so I asked how she was doing. She leveled with me. Things were not going well. Her doctor had suspended treatment and suggested she get in touch with a hospice. "What are you feeling and thinking right now?" I asked. "How are you handling this new development?"

"Well, I haven't been down this road before, so I'm trying to learn as much as I can about this final chapter of my life. I'm exploring life's last adventure," she confessed.

"What a compelling thought," I replied. "Let's make that the topic of this next seminar."

She was skeptical. "Will the church feel okay about offering that?" I assured her that the church should be eager to present a program about end-of-life planning. B. J. then asked, "Could we work on it together? It would be excellent therapy for me. I won't be here when you have the program in October, but I would like to be a part of your preparation."

I went to her home on a regular basis to discuss our plans. She had lost her hair and was pretty much confined to bed. I often sat alongside her, as we chatted about her life, her feelings, her family, and her childhood. We talked about her accomplishments, disappointments, pleasures, and unfinished business. We laughed and cried together.

B. J. died that July.

Notices were placed in the church bulletin about the October program. Reactions reflected the denial that pervades society. Some church members asked how in the world I could lead such a workshop.

My husband and I decided to present the seminar together. Jenks is a retired oil company marketing vice president, so he is an excellent planner and public speaker. We designed an interesting brochure that included the unique topics we'd be discussing. The pamphlet was available in the church office and mailed to other organizations.

Only five people preregistered for the seminar. We nevertheless felt the information was important enough to present to those courageous few. Forty people attended the first meeting. By the last session, one hundred were in attendance.

The seminars, a memorial to B. J. Frye, were hugely successful and took on a life of their own. We received requests from other churches. One presentation was given in Chicago. Other requests came from retirees clubs. I was asked to speak on this subject at the Cancer Patients' Conference sponsored by M. D. Anderson Hospital, a world-renowned cancer research center. We held a one-day seminar at the University of Houston tailored for professional caregivers.

The enthusiasm and questions raised in my seminars convinced me there was a need for a sensitive, candid, and uplifting book that readers would not find intimidating. Although my ten years as a newspaper columnist and my great interest in this subject encouraged me to take on the challenge, I was unaware of the huge task ahead of me, but I felt my goals for the book were worth any effort.

They are to

1. Motivate others to recognize the benefits and importance of being informed about end-of-life decisions.

2. Inspire everyone to prepare a personal end-of-life plan to

avoid the pitfalls that await the family if the deceased has not adequately prepared for this inescapable event.

3. Give hope to the survivors, equipping them with knowledge of what to do when a death occurs and assisting them in building bridges to the future.

4. Generate a sense of excitement about living to the fullest now.

Transition *from* life can be just as profound, intimate, and in some ways joyful as birth. Our daughter Toby observed, "Mom, instead of the Lamaze method for helping with birth, your book is the LaMargie method for dying, giving psychological insight and specific steps to lessen pain and increase comfort during one of the most stressful events in life."

I hope this book will be a source of power for everyone, providing enlightenment, humor, and common sense as you create the satisfaction that comes from making thoughtful plans for the end of your life.

1

SINCE YOU ONLY DIE ONCE . . . DO IT RIGHT

LOOKING AHEAD AT LOOKING BACK

Imagine the family scene immediately after your death if you leave no instructions for your final arrangements. What might it be like? Perhaps something like this?

> There is my grieving family down there, huddled around the breakfast table, looking through the phone book for funeral homes. Delores is crying hysterically. Cliff is taking over and dominating everybody like he always has. He's barking out orders about what to do first. Can't he see that Kevin and Delores need comforting?
>
> I wanted my body to be cremated and just have a simple service in the church. But now Megan is telling the others that she objects to cremation because it's against her religion. Guess I never discussed that idea with her. Why aren't they calling my pastor for help?
>
> Holy smoke! Now Cliff is calling the most expensive funeral home in the book. They can't afford that. What's he thinking?
>
> They are all arguing about how much to spend on a casket and what cemetery to use. Kevin is asking how they'll pay for everything. Hmm . . . Megan is shuffling through my desk

files looking for my will and any clues that might help with their decisions. She's wasting her time. She won't even find the name of my lawyer there.

They're all talking and nobody is listening.

Who will write my obituary? What's going to happen to my money and those special things I've collected during my lifetime? I can see a nasty fight coming. And none of them know about my real estate. That's sure to cause turmoil, especially in light of the information in my safe-deposit box. I wonder if they will even find it. I wish I had discussed more things with them—told them how much I loved them. Oops, I gotta go; time to get fitted for my wings.

MAKING A COMMITMENT

If you care about your loved ones and want to make your death easier for them, it is vital that your desires, decisions, and instructions be discussed with the important people in your life. Your choices should also be written out so they will be available when the time comes.

When you have done that, you will derive a deep sense of satisfaction, accomplishment, and relief about the future. Your loved ones will be grateful both now and after your death for all the effort you put into easing their grieving process.

Either intentionally or by neglect, most people choose to be *indecisive* in some areas of their lives. Preparing for death usually gets this treatment. You can change the way you think about this dilemma by making a *commitment* to begin the planning process for life's most overlooked milestone.

Your decision to take charge of life's last passage honors you and benefits everyone you care about. Leaving it to chance is a set-up for painful family chaos. Don't slam the door on your way out.

2

Thoughtful Planning Is
a Wonderful Gift

THE MORE YOU TALK ABOUT IT, THE EASIER IT GETS

Jenks and I were having a conversation in the family room with our daughter Susan, who is an attorney. "Why are you writing a book about death?" she asked. "I don't want to think about it."

We asked her what she would do if we both died and she was in charge of making all the funeral arrangements.

"Guess I'd just call the funeral home. Then I'd expect them to take over and do whatever needs to be done."

"How would you answer their questions about which minister at the church to notify, where we would be buried, what kind of funeral to have, what doctor to call to verify death, who should be notified, and what our obituaries would say?"

Susan was silent for a moment. "I never thought about all those decisions. In fact," she smiled, "I'm not planning on you two ever dying." She paused, then added, "I know you have an estate lawyer. Can't remember his name, but I have his card. You've told me about your broker and bank accounts. And the records are all in the bottom drawer of your desk labeled 'Going-Away File,' right?

"Are your wills still in the safe-deposit box along with copies of insurance policies and trust agreements? I remember you had all of us sign a card so, if necessary, any of us can get into the box. Another big question is funeral expenses. Financing has to be arranged in advance, doesn't it? And then what happens to all of your stuff? Like who gets the Santa Claus mugs you made years ago? Wow. Death is a jumble. So much to think about. So many decisions."

As we discussed these topics, Susan became more interested. "So what you are doing is putting your ideas into this book as a guide to planning for death. And if you discuss with us what you're recommending to your readers, then all of us kids will know what to do when you die. Makes sense. You really are doing it right. But how do *you* feel . . . organizing all this information and going to so much effort thinking about your own deaths?"

Aha, now it was her turn. She was asking *us* questions. Jenks and I thought carefully before responding.

"Death can be scary and terrifying. Especially thinking of each other dying, or for that matter, any of you kids. We know it will be a lot more traumatic than we can even imagine. We feel pressured to get things in order, hoping to reduce the anguish. Our research has been a wake-up call. It reminds us of the many end-of-life decisions that need to be made.

"But we are discovering that getting our lives in order and making the hard choices are satisfying. Putting documents in our 'Going-Away File' and telling you all where this important information is located gives us both a great sense of relief. And when we add something really important, we celebrate it. We hope this will make it easier for you to be better prepared for life's final chapter. Then we can relax and concentrate on enjoying the time we have left."

Susan reacted, "You know, at first it was upsetting to hear about all these things. But discussing it helps. Guess it's like anything. The more you talk about it, the easier it gets. What a wonderful gift!"

CREATING A MASTER FILE

How can you "straighten up and die right"? Lots of things should be considered. Like working on whatever goals you want to accomplish before you die. Remembering to treasure cherished possessions, then choosing people who will ultimately receive them after you're gone. Gathering your vital papers, including an updated will, and informing your significant others where they are filed.

Others things to consider include exploring the options concerning burial and funeral services and letting loved ones know your wishes so they can plan your going-away party with your desires in mind. Imagine what major life changes might occur later and think about how you can alter your lifestyle to accommodate them. Anticipate your final days, and let your family know how you hope to be cared for. This is a lot to keep track of, but all of these subjects will be discussed in the following chapters, with hints for organization and recordkeeping.

Of course some of these topics normally are not a lot of fun to chat about around the dinner table with your family and friends—or to read about in your leisure time at the beach. But I honestly believe, based on considerable personal experience and as a therapist, that taking the time and making the effort to *plan well* for your end-of-life adventure can be very rewarding and, in many ways, enjoyable.

And your thoughtful preparation does not *have* to be a huge or intimidating task. I suggest you try something as easy as this: Get some file folders and keep them handy as you read these pages. Then, simply write a subject name on a folder tab each time you come across an end-of-life topic on which you would like to collect information. Keep your folders in alphabetical order and you are on your way. Over time you will begin to convert the information you are gathering into a plan.

Suggested End-of-Life Planning Files

Advance Directives	Hospice
Attorney	Instant Action Folder
Bank Accounts	Insurance
Benefits	Inventory
Birth Certificate	Loans
Bodacious-Living Ideas	Long-Term Care Information
Bonds/Securities	Marriage License
Brokerage Accounts	Memorial Service
Burial Information	Military Papers
CPA	Mortgage Papers
Caregivers	Obituary
Cars/Vehicles	People to Notify
Cemetery Information	Real-Estate Titles
Cherished Possessions	Social-Security/Medicare Information
Church Contacts	Stages of Grief
Comforting Acts	Stocks/Mutual Funds
Contracts	Tax Returns
Deposit Box	"Ten-Best-Things" List
Divorce Papers	Things I Want to Do before I Die
Financial Statements	What to Do When Death Occurs
Funeral Home Information	Wills
Going-Away Party	

When you see magazine articles or news items that pertain to a related subject, or you just have a thought or questions about any of these topics, you will have an organized place to file them. Your folders can be kept in a file cabinet, a box, or a drawer. Or your computer may work best for you.

Naming your master file system makes it more personal and more fun. Some of our seminar attendees came up with creative names such as Last Hurrah; Up, Up, and Away; Vital Papers; Dead End; Finito; Last Passage; Final Exit; Finish Line; 19th Hole; To Die For; Over My Dead Body; and Last Expedition. One of my favorites was by someone who really applied some creativity to the whole package:

> **One for the money**—Organizing financial and legal information.
> **Two for the show**—Showing and discussing information with significant others.
> **Three to get ready**—Making end-of-life decisions.
> **Four to go**—Funeral planning. The end.

We call our master plan our "Going-Away File." Approaching the filing system with a touch of humor reminds us that this is only one part of the life that God has given us, and it can be embraced, not shoved aside.

THE HURDLE

Death is difficult. It eventually touches every family and is almost always unexpected, which is why planning ahead can make a difference. Far too few people appreciate what a wonderful gift thoughtful end-of-life planning can be. Without it, those left behind suffer not only grief and sadness, but they are often left with "sticker shock." Lack of preparation can leave them feeling emotionally and financially hijacked.

They feel like a door has been slammed shut.

Although some people seem to be more open to a discussion about death and dying, this subject is still pretty much taboo in many families—and many churches. It *is* hard to talk about it. When I suggested to my church that I lead a program on organizing life's final chapter, it caused quite a commotion. Some thought almost no one would attend. Eventually the church decided it was a good idea. The minister told me that most everyone needs help in knowing how to discuss final arrangements, but he was glad that I would be the leader of the seminar instead of him.

I got similar reactions outside the church as well. Once, when I called my answering service to get messages, the operator was reading off the names of people who had called when she suddenly gasped. "Oh my God," she said, "Someone called to ask about a seminar on death and dying and how to die right. I've never heard of such a thing."

At my seminars on making end-of-life plans, attendees are usually cautiously enthusiastic when they come in for the first session. They wonder if they will even be comfortable, much less enjoy, talking about death. One of the first things I do is invite them to share their expectations for the workshop, which gets them involved and broadens everyone's perspective. In the program we tell stories and even joke about death. And we reminisce about the deaths of others and preview our own until, believe it or not, it seems as if the skeptical souls have leaped some invisible sky-high hurdle that is now well behind them. And though, only minutes ago, there was doubt and hesitation, the room is now filled with a spirit of freedom, openness, and humor. Suddenly the participants find themselves enjoying the planning process. They are surprised to learn that there really are simple steps to follow in preparing for life's ending. They share experiences, both good and

bad, and we laugh together as they learn how to create a plan—
piece by piece.

PLEASE LISTEN TO ME

Some of the experiences the people shared were similar to the ones
my clients had shared with me in therapy. When Amelia, sixty-
eight, arrived in my office, she had been told she had six months to
live. But no one would talk with her about it. She was not morbid,
but wanted to relive old experiences; express her ideas about death;
and talk about where she would be buried, who should be notified,
and what favorite poems, hymns, and Bible verses she wanted in
her service. Sharing the history of antiques that filled her home
was important, as well as all those wonderful recipes she carried in
her head. She thought that people who know when they are going
to die have an edge. Amelia told me, "Letting go should be a celebration of life and love. I want to talk about my dying because
that's what I'm doing right now."

Amelia only wished her family would listen to her ideas. She
believed in a loving God and told me she felt the best was yet to
come. But her husband of forty-five years was so overcome with his
own grief about her dying that he was unable to carry on any
conversations about her life's ending. She mistook his silence for
anger. Her son scolded her for thinking the worst and not being
optimistic. Teenage grandchildren were uninterested in hearing
about her childhood on the farm in Wisconsin. Even her minister
suggested she should have faith and not talk about dying.

Family and friends sometimes think they are giving hope and
encouragement when they refuse to listen to a dying person
express concerns about death. Most everyone feels inadequate in
the face of a dying family member or friend. You may not know

what to say or what to do. You may hesitate to talk about either faith or fear; yet when you resist talking about a person's impending death, the message you send is "I don't care." Avoiding the subject, or substituting a phony upbeat attitude, can be confusing to a dying person. You can learn to feel comfortable talking about this subject.

As Amelia and I discussed her frustrations, she became more comfortable when she better understood the reasons for her family's reactions. She invited the whole family to our next session. They talked together about their feelings and concerns regarding Amelia's "last waltz," as she called it. Holding hands, they reflected on the life that they had shared, including special and amusing incidents. Laughter and tears helped them express Amelia's importance and assured her that she would be long remembered. Grief is only one aspect of death. Lifelong remembrances are lasting gifts.

Emotions and memories, however, aren't the only areas of life where neglect can have disastrous consequences. Blake was a young man whose wife died after a brief illness. He had little money and medical bills had swallowed up his savings, but he thought his wife deserved a special send-off to show his love for her. So he charged an expensive funeral on two credit cards. Now he is struggling to pay off a huge debt. By comparing costs at several funeral homes or talking to his wife about her desires, he could have planned a special send-off for about half the price he paid. Like most people, Blake was unwilling to explore funeral choices.

Unfortunately, Blake's story is not unusual. Donna's husband died after a five-year illness. During his last week's stay in the hospital, I suggested that she make some decisions about his burial. She resisted the idea because she thought such action would be disrespectful while her husband was still alive. When death came, Donna quickly arranged for a fancy mortuary to pick up the body. After visiting with the mortician she realized that cremation was her choice and other services were not needed. By that time, it was too late to change course. Her bill came to more than six thousand dollars to cover cremation and administrative fees. Afterward Donna wished she had explored other possibilities before her husband's death.

Wisdom is needed most and is often in short supply when death occurs in your own family. Absence of a preplanned, thoughtful closure to the dying process involves enormous repercussions for the survivors. Being informed about the complexity of decisions and the available possibilities enables you to make better choices. Acting on this knowledge quiets fears about what will happen to you and those you care about.

You only die once, but you will come back many times . . . in your loved ones' memories. How you leave this life can beautifully influence the memories of you that your survivors will experience after your death. Those thoughts can provide loving and pleasant recollections for years to come, or they can leave a stain on those remembrances. To be remembered well is one of the delicate treasures of immortality.

The healing power of end-of-life planning, before we say goodbye, can be a wonderful gift of love bestowed on all those whom you leave behind.

1. How many more years do you think you will live? How does your answer influence the need for planning your final chapter?
2. How will planning for the end of your life be helpful to you and your loved ones?
3. What are some end-of-life decisions you could make now?
4. What is the most difficult issue to discuss about your end-of-life decisions?
5. Who are the important people you will want to inform about your plans?
6. What does your family know now about your preferences for the end of your life?
7. What concerns you most about dying?
8. What memory of you would you like to leave behind? How can you best pass on such gifts as your wisdom, faith, and understanding of life?
9. If you were responsible for planning the closure on the life of a significant other, what information would be most helpful?

3

BEFORE I DIE, I WANT TO . . .

Life is full of things you *want* to do or *ought* to do . . . before you die.

If you are thinking about some pleasurable activities such as interesting trips, buying something you have always wanted, or getting together with special people, you are right on target. Give yourself some gifts of joy.

Chores are always waiting for you; sometimes more important tasks get pushed off the radar screen by work. Life is full of loose ends. Every year starts with new recordkeeping, added files, and other changes. No wonder you put off decisions about the things you ought to do before you die. There are so many things you must do to take care of living. In addition to your "gifts of joy" to your-self, think about other aspects of your life you've been putting off as well, such as cleaning up and organizing your vital papers. Even simple tasks can stir a world of memories and desires. So when is the right time to start a list of personal things you want to do or organize before your life's ending?

A few weeks after Mom's funeral in 1967, Dad announced, "I want to take care of some business. We need to look in the safe-deposit box and list what's there. Since I can't drive anymore, I don't get a chance to go to the bank. I have forgotten what all is in it. Nothing very important, but we should look it over. I've kept a few silver coins there, and I think the last letters from your brothers are in there, too. Maybe that's where I put my ten shares of Conoco stock. Wish I could have bought more when Jenks worked there before their stock went up. I think your mother's list of our possessions is in the box. She was an organized person. She wrote stories about each of the antiques we have in the house."

Our visit to the safe-deposit box was an emotional event. I had not been there before. As we sat in the little anteroom with the box open between us, Dad sorted through the items and explained their value to me. He shuffled through a group of pictures showing scenes from Beirut, the surrounding area, and a picture of him holding a mummy's hand that had been taken from an Egyptian tomb.

"My three years as a teacher in Syria, starting in 1910, was a unique experience, maybe the most significant event of my life. I always wished I could have gone back there for a visit."

Then from the bottom of the box, he lifted out a small church pledge envelope. He leaned back and laughed. "Looky here. This may be the most valuable thing in the safe-deposit box—my gold tooth."

Dad would smile to know that thirty years later we sold his gold tooth for two dollars.

After our bank visit, Dad sat at his roll-top desk and listed some things he wanted to do. Then he handed me a stack of address labels that he had torn off letters from old friends and relatives. "I want you to write these people about your mother's death and tell them I'd like to hear from them." He hadn't lost his ability to give me orders.

Dad was planning his Going-Away Party, taking charge, and

getting organized. He was sorting out things he wanted to handle before he died.

THINGS TO DO—WHEN TO START

I haven't a clue how old you are or the condition of your health or what accident awaits you around the next corner. But I have watched enough people die at every imaginable age, that I have no doubt whatsoever that you need to start planning now for the last chapter of your life. You and I both know, however, it is your job, and it can be started slowly, one step at a time, until all the projects are completed.

For example, consider the people you want to thank for their friendship and for what they have meant to you. What joy you can release by verbally saluting these folks! What surprises will come back to you? Wait and see. You will discover as much pleasure for yourself as for those who hear from you. Maybe more. Of course you can write love messages, but words also need to be spoken face to face.

Maybe you could be courageous. That's another word for caring enough to mend broken fences. I'm talking about those relationships that have become gritty and need some lubrication. A great victory awaits you when you heal hurts and offenses, ask forgiveness, and offer love. You know what needs to be done to improve your relationships. Mended friendships can generate harmony and peace of mind. When apologizing for hurtful actions, people often defend or explain their behavior, which can negate the effort. It is difficult not to do that. They want the other person to see their side of the situation. But justifying actions often wipes out all good intentions. If you need help in knowing what to say, try these magic words: "I hurt you. I was wrong. Please forgive me." And remember to say, "I love you and appreciate you."

On the more practical side, information such as financial records and the names of your attorney, executor, and accountant, along with their addresses and phone numbers, should be put on paper and discussed with significant others. All of these items are essential, and they are part of your vital papers to be discussed in chapter 4.

One of the most important things to do right now is to prepare a last will and testament. A will is the foundation for taking charge of your life and your death. In chapter 5 you will find more information on this important subject.

You might be one of those people with special reserved seats at the theater or sporting events. Those tickets can be passed on to someone who always wished they had such a close view of the action.

Then there are those mundane things you softly say to yourself, "I'll do it some day." Focus your attention now on the goals you want to accomplish. They may involve sorting out, cleaning up, and inventorying.

Pretty soon you will be relishing what you have accomplished—preparing for your final chapter and finding it surprisingly satisfying. You can add a lot of postscripts to your list of personal things you want to get done.

ADVANCE DIRECTIVES

Another big "ought to do" is to protect yourself and your family from potential suffering and excessive expenses by executing *advance directives*. The dramatic need for completing appropriate forms like the ones described below is evident in hospice research, which revealed that about 76 percent of adult Americans have not put in writing how they want to be cared for at the end of life.

The descriptions below are limited and provide general information only. The actual legal forms will vary from state to state.

Durable Power of Attorney: Delegates someone to act in your behalf.

"I designate _____ to act for me, make decisions on business and personal matters, and this document will be honored even if I later become mentally or physically incompetent."

Durable Medical Power of Attorney for Health Care: Appoints someone who can request or deny medical care if you become incapacitated.

"I name _____ as my agent who has authority to make any and all health care decisions, in accordance with my wishes, when I am no longer capable of making them myself."

Directive to Physicians (Living Will): Tells medical workers your wishes regarding life-sustaining care.

"If I have a disease or illness certified to be a terminal condition by two physicians and the application of life-sustaining procedures would only artificially prolong the moment of my death, I direct that such procedures be withheld or withdrawn and that I be permitted to die naturally."

Appointment of an Agent to Control Disposition of Remains: Names someone to be responsible for making decisions about what to do with your remains after your death.

"I name _____ as my agent who will have authority, upon my death, to make all decisions with respect to the disposition of my remains, in accordance with my wishes."

Appointment of a Guardian for Adult, Minor, or Disabled Children: Names a person to be guardian for your minor or disabled children.

"I appoint _____ as a guardian to make decisions, after my death, concerning minor or disabled children."

Out-of-Hospital Do Not Resuscitate Order (DNR): For the purpose of instructing emergency medical personnel or other health care professionals to forgo resuscitation attempts.

"If I am in a state of medical decline where there is no chance for my recovery, and death is imminent, I request DNR orders to be in place, with no resuscitation procedures to be used."

Legal copies of these forms may be obtained from an attorney, mortuary, hospital, or the American Medical Association. Questions can be asked about these forms and others by calling the Funeral Consumers Alliance at 1-800-765-0107. Other information can also be found on their Web site: www.funerals.org.

It is advisable to consult with your estate attorney to avoid possible conflicts with other documents when completing advance directives. If you have not already set up a file folder called "Advance Directives," do it now and add these documents to it.

WHAT SOME PEOPLE ARE DOING

In addition to a bit of recordkeeping and organizing your personal papers and possessions, plan those trips and visits to old friends for which you always said you never had the time. One retired couple bought an RV and traveled around the country visiting national parks. On each anniversary, a young couple made a ritual of discussing places they wanted to explore in the future. The list included surrounding areas as well as scuba-diving adventures in exotic places. A widowed grandmother had a goal of making quilts for her four grandchildren. A doctor became interested in tracing his ancestors and creating genealogy charts to give his family. He discovered his father had been married before and had another family that he knew nothing about.

An older couple made arrangements to donate their bodies to a medical school after their deaths and informed their children of their plan. A young father, who died unexpectedly at age thirty-seven, left his wife and two small youngsters a substantial life insurance policy along with love letters they found in his safe-deposit box. A young mother, ill with cancer, started a diary, in which she passed on to her children thoughts about her life, faith, and her hopes for their future.

One person told me after attending my seminar that she visited several funeral homes to gather information, collected and filled out legal directives, and updated her will. A middle-aged minister and his wife started a savings plan after their kids left home. When he died at age fifty-nine, they had accumulated a sizable amount, which was a wonderful gift for his wife.

Many of these folks started out just like Steve, however. While I was riding a stationary bicycle at the gym, Steve, a fellow biker, struck up a conversation. He had heard I was writing a book and asked about it. When I told him the subject, he frowned and said, "How depressing." I told him how much I enjoyed researching this project and that I have visits with cancer patients in my office nearly every day during which preparing for death is a common subject.

Steve said he was thirty-nine and thought it was a little early for him to be thinking about this subject. I told him about people

I knew who had died at various ages—children, young people, and older folks.

He said he had two children, aged eight and ten, then asked, "When is the right time to talk to kids about death?"

I replied, "When is the right time to talk to kids about sex?"

He laughed. "Are the two related?"

I told him they are related in that both topics need to be talked about and the sooner the better, but in terms appropriate to the ages of the children. You don't wait to tell your kids all about sex until they're ready to go out the door on their first date. Then I told him about two little girls whose fish had died and how I talked to them about death as it related to their pet.

He smiled, "I getcha. You know that's not a bad idea."

When I was leaving the gym, he called out, "I'd like to talk to you more about this subject sometime. Guess we never know when our last ride is over."

SUGGESTIONS FOR "THINGS-TO-DO" LIST

1. Prioritize a list of things to do. Revise the list on your birthday.
2. Strengthen relationships. Mend those that are broken.
3. Make a list of people you want to visit and those you wish would visit you.
4. Write letters or make calls.
5. Make important phone calls and discuss ideas about your final chapter with your family.
6. Organize files and write important letters.
7. Make a list of things about yourself you'd like to pass on to your children or grandchildren: memories, beliefs, and dreams, as well as possessions.

8. Become acquainted with and fill out appropriate advance directive forms.
9. Look over your possessions and get rid of things no longer needed or wanted.
10. Think about rewarding activities to participate in now.
11. Celebrate each accomplishment.
12. Live life to the fullest in the present.
13. Make a list of all your blessings.

4

YOUR VITAL PAPERS

Sometimes I have difficulty keeping up with my ordinary items, such as car keys, glasses, appointment calendar, and important notes. I do better when I remember to put such items in a convenient "special" place where I can find them easily.

The same is true for all essential paperwork. If something happened to you today, what discoveries will surprise your family as they search through your vital papers? Would your family know where to find your will, insurance policies, and bank records? Will they find all the important information they need? There ought to be a file called "special place," just so *you* can locate your missing stuff. Even husbands and wives in a good relationship do not always share essential information. Family members are often left in the dark trying to locate critical documents after a person dies. Planning ahead is a tremendous gift to your family.

ORGANIZED CHAOS

Many years ago my father-in-law, thinking he was saving money on taxes, kept his interest-bearing bank accounts below a certain amount and deposited money in various savings associations around northern Kentucky. But he failed to tell anyone the names of these institutions or their locations. After he died, his children were unable to find his records and had to call every financial organization in the area to see if he had an account there. Although he tried to be a responsible provider for his children, his hidden assets proved to be temporary liabilities.

Similarly, my father's Uncle Will, a doctor in Chicago, did not trust banks or any saving establishment because he thought they had cheated him. My parents were named executors of his will, and after he died at age eighty-four, they drove from Kentucky to his home in Chicago. There they discovered quantities of cash in surprising places: under the mattress, tucked into books, inside chair cushion covers, among bed linens in the closet, behind canned foods on pantry shelves, and in a jelly jar in the refrigerator. Mom and Dad rifled through every item in his home.

Later Dad chuckled whenever he retold the treasure hunt adventure. He thought Uncle Will, from his ringside seat in heaven, was having a hilarious time laughing at all the confusion he had created. Most likely he was also watching to see if all his money was found. But Uncle Will's treasure hunt is not an isolated story. Too often, families are forced into such hide-and-seek games after a death. Sometimes older people hide information about personal property and financial matters out of fear that it may cause problems among their heirs or even be abused in some way. They worry that advance knowledge of family financial affairs may create power struggles among their children. Or they fear that someone who is entrusted with confidential details may secretly withdraw money or hide it from the other family members. There are those who fear crucial data could be used against them. For example, if there is an awareness of a lot of money in the family, children might demand or expect parents to pay their debts or provide them with a higher standard of living. Some fear they may be robbed or have their lives threatened.

Not all heirs need to know all the financial details, but at least one person should be informed about the locations of the will, other vital documents, and the names of your executor and attorney.

Being informed is crucial. Some married couples I have counseled tell me that they have no idea what is in the joint income-tax form they sign. There are spouses who illegally sign a partner's name on legal documents. I encourage everyone to become more responsible and better-informed and to ask questions about all legal matters.

Too often people do not update their official papers by changing wills, beneficiaries, and financial records as circumstances shift. The failure to keep records current creates confusion and can result in disaster. One of my clients, who was separated from her violent husband, changed her will to make her supportive brother the beneficiary. Unfortunately, this woman died before signing the new document. Based on the old will, her abusive husband was the sole heir to her estate.

Like most people of my generation, I grew up in a culture where talk of family finances was a no-no. The "don't ask, don't tell" environment seemed to have been invented by my family. I didn't have a clue about money or how much it cost to live. When I was ready to go away to school, Dad informed me I could attend any college where I could work my way through. His offer sounded like a great opportunity. I was in charge.

But trouble struck when I applied for a job at Eastern Kentucky State College in Richmond. While filling out the required job application form, questions about my family income led to a catastrophic situation. I had two older married brothers. Bobby was in the Army Air Corps and Johnny was in the Naval Air Force. They must make a lot of money, I thought. My older sister, Fran, was a flight attendant with American Airlines, so I knew she was doing well. Dad was a substitute teacher. Since we lived in a brick home, I thought our family was richer than most of my friends. So on the application form, I guessed our family income in 1941 to be one hundred thousand dollars. (Much later I learned that Dad made twelve hundred dollars a year.) Whether my income estimate was a little or a lot, I had no idea—until the dean of students called me into his office. He said I was not a candidate for college jobs because of my family's high income. I cried. I begged to be allowed to stay in school.

While I sat in his office, the dean called my family. Bobby, home on leave from the Air Corps, volunteered to drive down to the college, two hours away, and straighten things out. Nervously holding the phone to my ear, I heard, "Don't worry, Little Shrimper; I'll take care of it." ("Little Shrimper" had become my older brothers' pet name for me.) Just hearing his voice, I knew everything would work out okay. A job as the college post-office manager allowed me to stay in school.

I'm not suggesting that kids need to know every financial detail. But I think it's helpful, in case of emergencies, to share enough information that everyone is generally acquainted with the family state of affairs. At some point, and it varies with the circumstances, most adult children should be reasonably informed about family finances and recordkeeping for their own peace of mind. And spouses need to be fully informed. I am aware of a situation where a wife did not get proper medical help for her very sick husband because she thought they could not afford it. He died. You know the rest of the story . . . They had plenty of money.

ORGANIZING YOUR VITAL PAPERS

Too often people have their vital papers scattered in many places. They may be in a file cabinet in the basement, at the office, in a safe-deposit box, on a shelf in the attic, in the computer, or in boxes stacked in a closet or the garage. Or in all of the above. This arrangement may be satisfactory for you because you know where most things are kept, but finding everything may be impossible for anyone else. Major problems will occur if you have a crippling stroke or, by some other tragedy, lose your ability to communicate. It will be truly disastrous if no one knows what vital information and documents you have and where you keep them.

In our home Jenks and I have separate filing systems in our desk drawers. We think we are quite well organized but sometimes are at a loss trying to find something in the other person's files. Jenks keeps the car file in his desk, but when I tried to find my car insurance information, it wasn't there. Turns out it is in the insurance file. Makes sense. I just didn't know his system.

The goal of this chapter is to encourage you to organize and simplify your recordkeeping system to minimize problems. One of the best ways to do this is to create a master file system that is complete, well labeled, and familiar to your spouse and at least one other person, like your executor, accountant, or attorney.

If you have started a Going-Away File (or whatever you named yours), you won't need a separate vital papers system. Just put each of your documents in a folder, label it so it can be easily identified, and place it alphabetically in your Going-Away File.

For example, you can have one category called "Insurance" in the *I* section of your master file. You might include folders that are labeled "Insurance—Accident," "Insurance—Auto," "Insurance—Health," "Insurance—Home." So if you or others ever have to search for information relating to any kind of insurance, the information would be filed in alphabetical order under *I* in your Going-Away File. Some folks may need only one folder named "Insurance" to hold all their insurance-related material.

Additional folders may be labeled "Tax Returns," "Investments,"

"Bank Accounts," "Mortgages," or any of your vital papers. Each one should, of course, be filed in alphabetical order.

There is something very satisfying about creating an organized filing system where you can easily find what you want. And when you come across magazine articles, newspaper clippings, or just have thoughts or questions that you write down about a topic, you will have a ready place to store them for future reference.

One color-conscious woman told me, "Organizing files like this is very important, but it's not my bag. So I make the project more inviting by using brightly colored folders and colored labels. My box of files is really pretty, and I look forward to adding new colors as I alphabetize my Going-Away File."

I hope you are already sensing that having an end-of-life master file system will give you the satisfaction of being in control as well as the comforting assurance that you are providing a thoughtful gift for your heirs.

I hear many unfortunate tales that result from unforeseen situations, carelessness, poor recordkeeping, and the propensity for privacy. A family in our neighborhood recently experienced a major crisis over the terminal illness of the father, who was kept alive by machines. Anger, guilt, fear, denial, and helplessness froze this loving family's decision-making ability over the issue of removing their father's life-support system. No preplanning instructions existed to settle this emotional issue. Their father died in a coma after many months (apparently not knowing anyone and unconscious of the dilemma that surrounded him).

CREATING YOUR INSTANT ACTION FOLDER

No matter how well prepared one is for the death of a loved one, it is always an incredibly profound and mystical experience. It is inevitable, yet somehow still seems impossible. Then it happens and the ones left behind have to start doing things. But what? And what should be done first?

This is where your Instant Action Folder comes in. If you could only have one folder in your Going-Away File, this should be the one. Its purpose is to list brief, essential actions that will be necessary immediately after your death. The objective is to give your survivors an instant plan so they can calm themselves, get help promptly, and take the steps you prefer for completing the ritual accompanying your death.

The form labeled "Instant Action Folder" below may be copied for your personal use. I have listed the information that should be included. This folder should be set apart from any others both by making it a different color and by keeping it in the front of your Going-Away File. Your spouse and at least one other person should know where you keep it.

Our folder is red and labeled in bold letters "Instant Action Folder—In Case of Death." It is the first folder in our Going-Away File. All of our children know where to find this folder.

Since my husband and I are in total agreement with the way things will be handled at the time of our deaths, we have only one Instant Action Folder, and it has only one page for each of us. Some couples will need separate folders if they differ on this matter.

Use the following form as a guide to set up your one-page Instant Action Folder. Add any details you think will be useful to your survivors in those first few hours after your death.

INSTANT ACTION FOLDER FORM

Immediate Information Required at Time of Death
1. Family members to notify (names and phone numbers).

2. Minister and place of worship to call.
3. Two close friends to call immediately to support survivors (names and phone numbers).
4. Hospice phone number (if one has been involved).
5. Name and phone number of the person who has authority to make decision about who to call to pick up the body.
6. Funeral home name and phone number to call to remove the body. (Note: In case of unusual circumstances—accident, crime, or suicide—the coroner or sheriff's office should be called.)
7. Burial instructions—mortuary services that will be needed.
8. Doctor's name and phone number to certify death.
9. Name and phone number of personal attorney, CPA, and life insurance agent.
10. Where additional information can be found.

Signed _____ Date _____

WALLET CARD INFORMATION

It is important to carry at all times a wallet card with emergency information. Your wallet will be the first place someone will look if you are incapacitated and unable to communicate.

One Friday morning our friend George was playing tennis with his usual foursome when his partner, Matthew, dropped his racket and sank to the ground. With help, he was able to walk to a nearby bench, but he couldn't talk. The first thing George did was look in his partner's wallet to try to find the telephone number of Matthew's wife. There were no phone numbers, so George accompanied his friend in an ambulance to a nearby hospital. It was there that the doctors learned that Matthew had suffered a minor heart attack. Matthew's wife still would have been unaware of what was happening had not one of the tennis players found her number in the records at the tennis club. A card such as the one shown here would have made it possible for her to be at the hospital before the ambulance arrived.

FRONT

Name: _____

Address: _____

In case of emergency, call: _____

Phone: _____

Doctor's name: _____

Doctor's Phone: _____

BACK

Allergies: _____

Health Problems: _____

Medications: _____

Blood Type: _____

Medical Insurance: _____

When Tomorrow Comes

When tomorrow comes . . .
I'll fly to the moon.
Stare at the stars
From the tip of Mars.
Make ports of call
To the galaxy all.

When tomorrow comes . . .
I'll sing the old songs
While dancing all night long.
I'll watch movies of Kong
Eat popcorn till dawn
Helping someone belong.

When tomorrow comes . . .
I'll write my next book.
Cast a stone
In the nearby brook.
Go for a look
In the tiniest nook.

But what about today
Before comes the gray?!
Do I sadly say
There's no time to play??
No! I'll spread my wings
Shout hooray and soar away!!

—SYNTHA TRAUGHBER WEST, PH.D.
Today's Dreams, Tomorrow's Realities
Tyler, Texas

5

WILL POWER

Jim and his wife came to me, filled with questions and mixed emotions. Jim's father, a lawyer, was one of those superorganized men. Everything was always in its place. Tools hung in their special positions on the wall of his workshop, desk drawers were immaculate, and his clothes were arranged in the closet according to color. For years, his father had told Jim that all his legal documents were complete and in place. Then last summer, while Jim and his wife were vacationing in Canada, his father died. They returned home immediately—relaxed in the knowledge that all the legal documents were current and organized.

While examining the will, they found that his dad had left everything to Jim's mother . . . who had died ten years before.

They came face to face with how a well-thought-out and up-to-date will might have left behind more pleasant memories. Such preparation is a matter of *will* power.

Jim and his wife spent several sessions with me working out their frustration and talking about how they could prevent similar problems for their own heirs. At the end of this chapter, you will find a summary of their ideas.

This chapter is designed to encourage you to develop and execute a thoughtful will. I am not an attorney, so I will not be giving you legal advice. But I will be trying to motivate you to do all the necessary planning and engage all the legal advisers you need for leaving your heirs the gift of a comprehensive and effective will.

WHY HAVE A WILL?

Will you allow strangers to take over your assets, spend your money without regard to your wishes, wastefully send the government extra sums of your hard-earned cash, decide what your children should receive, and pay potentially large professional fees for handling your affairs? That can happen, if you don't have a valid will. Would it shock you to learn that about 70 percent of American adults do not have a will? It should. An old proverb says, "A man who dies without a will has lawyers as heirs."

Everyone over the age of eighteen, especially those who are married or have children, should have a will (sometimes referred to as a "last will and testament"). Many people mistakenly believe that a will is unnecessary if their estate is small. But it is the only way that you, rather than a court, can name your executor (the person who will be responsible for making sure the things you leave behind will go to the people of your choice). Without a will, a court rarely distributes assets the way the deceased would have preferred. If there is no will, a court, not your heirs, could determine the custody of your minor children. And the laws of most states provide more adequately for surviving children than they do for the surviving spouse.

In one state a young husband died without a will, and his four young children inherited the bulk of his estate. The surviving wife had to hire an attorney and go to court to resolve the problem of supporting her family. That was not what the father intended. The result was emotionally traumatic and unnecessarily expensive.

Without a will, the details of an estate can keep survivors entangled for months, even years, sorting out the administrative minutiae and struggling with touchy decisions. These tedious chores complicate the grieving experience and delay emotional recovery. Poor planning can seriously erode your assets, which will reduce what is left for your heirs.

A will is the cornerstone of your estate planning and should simplify the probate process for survivors. It should furnish the basis for how you want to provide for those left behind. It should be proof of your thoughtfulness, purveying an orderly transfer of your estate assets with minimum taxes, probate costs, and administrative expenses.

DEFINITIONS

Definitions are often misunderstood or misinterpreted. When I was little, the Sunday school teacher told the Bible story about the publican and the sinner. Since I knew my mother was a Republican and my father was a Democrat, I assumed the story was about her; therefore, Dad must be the sinner.

I hope these few simple definitions will not be as confusing to you as my Sunday school lesson was to me. Knowing the meaning of legal terms will be helpful when preparing a will and thinking about estate planning.

Estate is a legal term that refers to a person's total property, such as your house, car, IRAs, etc. It also includes your liabilities and obligations, such as home mortgages, contracts, debts, or loan guarantees for others. In brief, it is everything you own and everything you owe.

Will is a document that states what you want to happen to your property after your death. Wills are normally typed, witnessed, and notarized. Most states honor handwritten wills that meet their requirements.

Executor is a person you name to carry out the instructions in your will. He or she will pay your debts and taxes, out of your assets, and manage your estate until it can be delivered to your heirs. Some persons die without writing a will or naming an executor. Then the court takes over.

Probate refers to official proof that your will is genuine. A person's executor brings the will before a probate court where the process for transferring ownership of your assets begins. If no executor has been named, the probate court appoints an administrator to process the estate. This procedure is more expensive and can greatly reduce the amount that heirs will eventually receive.

Interim Funds are temporary monies from your estate that are made available to your family between the time of your death and the settlement of your estate. Since the probate process can take up to a year or more, the family (or the executor) may need funds for paying bills and living expenses until final disbursements are made.

Living Trust is a legal entity you can create that is independent, separate, and self-contained. It holds assets you transfer to a trustee, someone you appoint (such as a bank, attorney, or yourself) for management, protection, and ultimate distribution. Trusts are used to keep assets out of probate court and for possible tax savings or tax deferment, protection of assets, and estate planning. They usually require professional help to establish and administer. Because of the complexity of laws in some states, instead of writing a will, estate lawyers use living trusts.

MAKING A WILL

Since estate laws are complicated, it is best not to use a do-it-yourself will. But if you can't do it any other way, rather than have no will at all, it is better to use a published form available at most office supply stores. Or you may simply handwrite your will and have your signature witnessed by two people and notarized. (Some states require two witnesses of your signature and some states require three.) You can buy computer software that will help you write a will. One of the best is WillMaker 8 Pro.

Remember to include a caring message of love and explanation to make these papers less formal. Consult, of course, with your attorney to make sure these words of kindness do not impinge on legal issues.

Nelson, the father of a close friend, died recently. After the funeral, his three adult children and his second wife gathered for the reading of his will. This father left his modest estate to his second wife without even mentioning his children's names. The message they inferred from him was, "You have not been important to me." His rejection will be a lasting memory, slamming a door that may never reopen. In some cases, a surviving spouse has a greater financial need than the children, but that explanation should be communicated before death or put in the will or a letter. When death comes, survivors need to be remembered lovingly. The legacy of kind words is often more meaningful than money. And may be your greatest gift.

Assuming that you choose to use legal counsel to create your will, here's how the process might work.

SELECT YOUR ATTORNEY

If your estate is small and uncomplicated, it is likely that a good general law or family law practitioner can service your needs adequately at a reasonable cost.

If your estate is large or complex, you need a certified estate-planning specialist in the state where you live. The field of law is like medicine in that it is highly specialized. You do not want a personal injury attorney to write your will and set up your family trusts any more than you would like a brain surgeon to perform your knee replacement. Engage a competent attorney whose area of expertise includes wills, trusts, and probate issues in your state.

There are, however, several very important qualifiers in your selection process. Integrity is important in any working relationship, but it is doubly critical in selecting your attorney. Before interviewing estate lawyers, get several recommendations from people you respect.

When calling to set up an appointment, ask if the initial interview is free. That is usually the case. Meet personally with the attorney to determine whether there can be an air of trust between the two of you. Be up-front about the size and complexity of your estate, and give the attorney a general idea of how you plan to distribute your assets. This information is needed to determine what will be charged. It is important to know the cost early so as to prevent the waste of everyone's time. Finally, you should decide whether this is an attorney whose style of communication you can easily follow. Don't place your will into the hands of a lawyer you don't understand.

INFORM YOUR ATTORNEY

After deciding on an attorney, you will need to provide detailed information. Usually that will include things like (1) a list of your assets and liabilities with their current market value, including your IRAs, benefit plans, life insurance, etc.; (2) your division and designation of assets to your beneficiaries; and (3) the name and information regarding your executor. Put down on paper what appeals to you as the best way to leave your estate in an orderly, loving fashion, selecting your choice of heirs. Your attorney will discuss what you want to do and can then make constructive suggestions on how to achieve your goals. Without exchanges of this nature, bizarre things can happen to the final settlement.

An attorney told me about a client who had been married three times but had never gotten around to changing beneficiaries on his retirement plans. When he died, most of his assets went to a former wife. Since his last wife of twenty years was not named as a beneficiary, she received very little from his estate.

Discussing your will and its contents with family members before you die may help alleviate problems after you are gone. In one family, Kellie, the only daughter, discovered after her father's death that he had left a $50,000 insurance policy to her that was unknown to any of his children and was not mentioned in the will. He had lived with her during his last years. And she had also been the primary caregiver of her deceased mom who had been terminally ill with cancer. Kellie's father had wanted to repay her for all she had done.

But that decision created major dissension among her siblings. Kellie was no longer invited to family functions. She was accused of bribing her parents into buying the insurance policy. Her children were banned from get-togethers with cousins. The relationships within the family were damaged forever. Kellie felt guilty, angry, sad, and helpless to change the way her brothers treated her. She told me, "I feel punished for caring for our parents when my brothers were unwilling to help."

Perhaps there was nothing this father could have done to change his sons' attitudes. But if he had talked with an attorney about his plan, the situation could have been different. An attorney might have suggested that the father explain to the boys: "Since Kellie took care of your mother and me during our closing years, I am leaving her an insurance policy to thank her for all she has done during a difficult period. It will help to offset the many expenses and loss of income she incurred on our behalf. I know you are grateful to her for making our last years easier for the whole family."

When considering whom to name as your executor, it can be helpful to look at your estate as a company. Whether it's large, small, or in between, ask yourself what kind of person you would like to be your president. It should be someone you trust; take into account such qualities as integrity, faith, competence, loyalty, compassion, and whatever else is important to you in this job description.

Of course, in addition to having the qualities you want, this person must be someone who is willing and able to devote time and diligence in following through with the necessary paperwork that must be accurately completed. He or she may be a family member or friend or, perhaps, your attorney, CPA, or bank officer. Discuss your will and intentions with the person you choose to handle your estate so questions can be answered and issues clarified. It is helpful to write out your intentions for the executor. Give the selection careful thought and prayer; your decision could have long-lasting consequences.

Compensation for executors is sometimes set by law and is paid out of the estate. Frequently executors who are close friends or relatives decline fees, but they deserve some payment because of the amount of work required in settling your estate.

My father was asked to be the executor for two elderly sisters who lived in Southgate, Kentucky. Dad was highly respected and known for his integrity, so he was often asked to handle various personal matters for people in the community. I was maybe ten years old when he told me he was going to walk across town to talk with these ladies about their wills. They lived in a little white frame house with a picket fence around their small yard. I wondered why a will was necessary for them because I thought wills were only for rich people.

These ladies called Dad often because they would change their minds and wanted him to advise them. It became a joke in our family that Dad seemed to spend a lot of time with these aging sisters. When they died, everyone was surprised to learn they left a rather large amount of money to the local public school. Dad knew what they were planning to do, and he refused to accept any payment for his work as executor.

REVIEW THE DRAFT OF YOUR WILL

Reading over the draft of your will and talking to a family member, your attorney, or executor can help you spot any glitches—things to change, add, or delete. Review the draft until you understand it and are satisfied that it says what you want it to say.

Just before he died, Ambrose Bierce wrote, "Death is not the end; there remains litigation." Family involvement in the draft of your will might reduce the probability of this bit of humor becoming a reality among your heirs. But that is not always the case.

Another attorney recalled the story about a single mother, who had a "no-good" son. This man was thirty-seven, did not work, and had been in trouble with the law on several occasions. The attorney suggested she not tell her son that she planned to put her assets into a trust that would manage his inheritance, and that he would not receive a large sum of money when she died.

Despite the lawyer's warning, she told her son about her decision. He exploded and told her that unless she changed her plan, he would make her life miserable and never speak to her again. She called the lawyer and changed her plan.

You should carefully consider both the circumstances and the individual personalities in your family in the process of determining whether to discuss your will with them before your death.

REVIEW, REVISE, AND SIGN YOUR FINAL WILL

Our experience has been that we revised our wills after reviewing the preliminary drafts, then we had more questions. Our attorney used a blackboard in his conference room to draw diagrams to explain how our trusts would function and how our estates would flow out to the beneficiaries.

When we were ready to sign the final documents, he called in two of his associates to witness and notarize our signatures. We felt a great sense of accomplishment and went to lunch to celebrate.

PUT YOUR WILL IN A SAFE PLACE

After signing your will, put it in a safe place known to your executor. A safe-deposit box should be used only if significant others have signed the required forms at the bank where the box is located, allowing them immediate entry after your death. Bank personnel check obituaries daily and safe-deposit boxes are locked after death notices appear in the paper. Access is denied to anyone except those who have signed the bank's required forms. Otherwise a court order is required to open the box, which can be very inconvenient. Some people place their legal documents in a special drawer in the house or office. The family or executor should know the location of all documents needed to process your will. Your attorney should keep a signed copy in case you lose the original or it is destroyed.

CHANGE YOUR WILL WHEN NECESSARY

One way to prevent mix-ups after your death is to review your will on a regular basis. When major changes occur, such as births, deaths, marriages, divorces, or inheritances, it is important to correct your will and make necessary changes to coincide with your present situation and desires. Your update should include beneficiaries, insurance, IRAs, retirement plans, and any other legal documents that have come about during the time since you first established your will. Small changes can make a huge difference and can usually be made inexpensively through a legal attachment called a codicil.

Alice married an eighty-year-old widowed neighbor who lived on a farm in western Kansas. He promised her that she could live on the farm for the rest of her life. When he died, she discovered that his will named his son as the sole heir to the farm. Since the son was not happy that his father had married Alice, he took over the land and she ended up having to leave the property.

Another common problem is invalidating a will by writing on the document or crossing out material. If you are considering changes in a signed and legal will, instead of marking on the original, make a copy. Make your notes on the copy, keeping the original unaltered. This way your will remains fully legal if you should die before having a new will signed and notarized.

ESTABLISH AN INTERIM FUND

What will happen financially between your death and the settlement of your will? That intervening time can create problems for those left behind. There are expenses that have to be met, and family members often do not have access to sufficient funds needed to pay for necessary items. Besides funeral and burial costs, there might be charges for a hospital, nursing home, medical care, and childcare. In addition, travel expenses may occur—not only at the time of death but also during the period prior to death when out-of-town family members want to visit. There are always unforeseen expenses that must be covered.

Even without a will, courts are usually lenient toward survivors' interim needs, but complications and time delays are common and may put an extra burden on those left behind. In community property states, this might be less of a problem. However, separate bank and savings accounts for each person can relieve this situation by making funds immediately available to the surviving spouse without going through probate. You can also buy a small life insurance policy on each spouse to provide immediate funds. In most cases an estate can be settled within a year. But whatever time it takes, interim financial obligations may be critical.

LIVE BODACIOUSLY

After you have completed your will, I hope you will walk out of your attorney's office, relax, and take a deep breath. Then celebrate and live bodaciously, knowing you have simplified the grieving process for your heirs and expressed your love to those left behind.

Remember Jim—whose "organized" father left everything to his deceased wife? Here are the guidelines Jim and his wife set for preparing a will:

1. Commit to preparing a will and updating it when changes occur.
2. Prepare a list of assets and decide how to distribute them in your estate plan.

3. Get professional help in preparing your will.
4. Make a separate written memorandum of people to receive special sentimental items that may not have a significant monetary value. A written list outside your will is easier and less costly to redo.
5. If possible, talk to family members together and give them a general idea of what is in your will so there will be no surprises.
6. Arrange for interim funds to cover expenses between the time of death and the distribution of assets.
7. Put these documents in your Going-Away File.

6

YOUR CHERISHED POSSESSIONS

Who gets the mummy's hand when you die?" was a question often asked of my dad by his grandkids. He brought this coveted treasure back from the Middle East in 1913, when he returned after three years of teaching at the Syrian Protestant College in Beirut, Syria (now the American University of Beirut in Lebanon). During a holiday journey to Egypt, his tour guide dug among the remains of a tomb they were visiting—a common practice then, although the idea would be appalling today. The mummy's hand caught Dad's eye. The guide offered him a deal. If my father would take his eleven-year-old daughter as a bride, the mummy's hand would be the dowry. Instead of taking advantage of that opportunity, Dad bought the petrified artifact for the equivalent of ten cents.

Not everyone grew up with a mummy's hand in the closet, but most people have important items among their possessions that have special significance—particular things that engender warm memories, are symbols of a family story or ancestor, or for whatever reason, they just happen to like.

Treasured items, when passed on to others, create opportunities within families to connect the past with the future. It is like bearing the torch between generations. Possessions are often a reflection of who you are, your value systems, and priorities, and they can represent more than just "things." A lovingly marked and treasured Bible can represent a grandparent's complete devotion. A handmade chest can be a reminder of a father's love and willingness to work hard for his family. As people change, objects that do *not* change become anchors to the past. Valued possessions may be part of this temporary earth, but they can carry on a sense of history, of love, of faith long after the people they represent are gone.

The purpose of this chapter is to encourage you to (1) identify *what* items among your possessions have major significance to you and why, (2) record *who* you want to receive them, (3) decide *when* you want to pass them on, and (4) determine *how* you want to distribute your treasured belongings.

WHAT ARE YOUR CHERISHED POSSESSIONS?

People often take their belongings for granted and fail to appreciate the satisfaction they bring. I'm not talking only about high-dollar items like houses, cars, boats, and jewelry but such things as certain lamps, rings, pictures, important letters, family Bibles, and photograph albums that generate good feelings and happy thoughts. Specific articles become cherished for a variety of reasons: how they were acquired, who the previous owners were, or because of meaningful events associated with them. And some hobbies and collections become valued possessions, such as model trains, art, coins, or stamps.

After my father-in-law died, his children looked for the small gold coin that he always carried in a hidden compartment in his wallet. They all knew the story behind this personal effect and had their wishful eyes on it. Many years earlier, Pop Jenkins had performed some free legal service for a "down-and-out" client who was so appreciative that he had given the coin as a gift. The one-dollar gold piece, smaller than a dime, was treasured because it was unique and had been kept as a reminder of a meaningful relationship. My husband and his two sisters drew straws to determine who would get this cherished possession. Jenks's twin sister became the proud new owner of the coveted keepsake.

Identifying your cherished possessions can be satisfying. What would you include? Where might you begin? I decided to start by making a list of those items that I value most—or that represent who I am—that I want to treat separately from the multitude of my belongings. This required walking through the house, into closets, the garage, wherever I have articles stored or just sitting around.

You may want to sit at your desk or breakfast table and think about all those things that are meaningful to you. Or recapture the pleasure by looking around your home and identifying cherished personal possessions. Open drawers; check out the kitchen cabinets and bookshelves. Are there particular paraphernalia at some other location . . . your office, safe-deposit box, or vacation home?

Mom's tall, cherry desk, one of her precious possessions, is in my office where it keeps me company and generates intimate childhood memories. I almost forgot to add it to my list.

With the aid of a notepad, a computer, or a tape recorder, make an inventory of your significant items and write or record the story behind each one. It was rewarding for me to relive the moments during which I acquired each article. I also took pictures of these possessions to include with their stories. Thus, what may seem to some to be merely a piece of furniture becomes part of my legacy to my family and friends.

WHO WILL RECEIVE YOUR CHERISHED POSSESSIONS?

After listing your cherished possessions, think of the various people in your family to whom you would like to give your treasures. It can be fun and gratifying to choose new owners who would get exceptional pleasure from your generosity.

There is no set formula for doing this. Perhaps the simplest method is just to write the recipient's name alongside each item on your cherished possessions list. Be sure to attach stories, histories, and other meaningful input about each one.

When I was making my own record, cheerfully assigning family names to each prize, I realized this opportunity deserves a lot more thought. It turned out there are a number of people besides my relatives that I want to remember and whom I want to remember me. This process took some serious consideration, but it became a pleasurable experience, remembering all of my valued friends, and knowing that I would be enhancing lasting connections. I included some folks I barely know who have done thoughtful things for me through the years. This process was interesting and satisfying, but also a little frustrating. I am still working on what to give to some people and when I want to part with certain things.

Giving special items to family, neighbors, and friends can create loving memories of you. Shortly after my Aunt Ora died at age ninety-four, a neighbor came to her house and asked me if there was anything she could have as a remembrance. I gave her the chair that she had admired and often sat in when having tea with my aunt.

WHEN TO GIVE AWAY YOUR CHERISHED POSSESSIONS

Very simply, you have two basic time frames for giving away your possessions—before you die or after you die. Of course, you will have more control, and probably more enjoyment, if you share your cherished things before you die. An old saying is "He who gives while he lives knows where it goes." If you choose to designate people to receive your treasures after your death, be sure to make a list and let your executor know about it.

The timing for passing on your possessions is a very personal decision. Uncertainties concerning when to part with your belongings can cause problems. Questions include "Will I miss the item or wish I still had it? Will the receiver appreciate it as much as I do?" If you feel overly anxious about giving away certain articles, you probably are not ready to part with them. Keep them—and give away the other things on your list when you are ready.

Part of your discomfort may be that you're wondering if your personal effects will be cared for after you give them to someone. Well, you can't be sure. One of the harder lessons in life is that you can't control what others do with gifts. But if choices are not made, the risk is even greater. Your possessions have a better chance of being valued when you choose where you want them to go than if someone else determines their ownership after you are gone.

At one seminar I led on this subject, Lucy, a new grandmother, shared a predicament. "When our first grandson was born, I gave his mother, my daughter-in-law, our son's silver baby spoon and other special childhood items, like his toys and books. She sold them in a garage sale. I was heartbroken. Those meaningful gifts from our past meant nothing to her. I wished I had kept them for one of the other children who would have valued them."

Lucy was upset by her daughter-in-law's lack of appreciation. For her to get on with their relationship, she needed to let go of her expectation. Different priorities should be respected. Giving gifts with a *tail* (an expectation) attached usually creates hard feelings and disappointments. I suggested to Lucy that she write about her anger at the situation and put on paper all the bad feelings she was holding on to. Writing is one way to get feelings out of your system and be freed up to live more peacefully. Such letters don't need to be mailed, but the process can be helpful. The goal is to give for the love of giving, then let go. Try not to waste energy fretting about things that can't be changed. Lucy needed to decide which she valued more—the gifts she had freely passed along or her relation-ship with her daughter-in-law.

Letting go of cherished possessions (and not so cherished items) carries with it a sense of simplifying life. Many years ago, while visiting my parents in Kentucky, they insisted we take their upright piano back to our home in Kansas City. Later Mom told me it was such a relief to have it gone, since neither of them played it anymore. She enjoyed rearranging the living room furniture and rehanging pictures that gave their home a fresh new look. And she no longer had to dust the piano keys. We all thought her living room seemed larger and a lot more inviting.

After forty years of enjoying the piano, we went through the same process. We were moving into a smaller home and needed to part with this cherished possession. Our children either had their own pianos or had no room for this one. A handyman who helped us around the house noticed the piano and asked about it. I told him I wanted to give it to someone who would appreciate and enjoy it. He smiled and said, "That's me. Our six-year-old daughter is just begin-ning piano lessons, and we would love to have it." Before he picked it up the next day, I sat on the old piano bench where Dad and the four of us kids would sit while he played all the familiar church songs and we would sing and laugh. I played the same tunes: "The Battle Hymn of the Republic," "Jesus Loves Me This I Know," "The Lord's Prayer." I played church camp songs and Girl Scout songs.

A flood of memories came back to me, and I found myself crying as I remembered all the lessons I had learned around this piano-lessons of faith, family values, humor, and Christian love. Then I wrote a letter to the new owners telling them the story of the piano. I told them this piano loved children, and I hoped it would give them lots of fun family times together. I tucked the note in the piano bench and lovingly sent it off to its new home.

You probably know people who can't part with anything during their lifetime. They leave everything to be distributed after they die. That is understandable when their possessions create a sense of significance, warmth, and security. But it is not nearly as gratifying . . . for them or their loved ones. Those who receive your possessions directly from your loving and generous hands—and hear you tell their stories—will feel their gifts have an added value.

Yet understanding why people drag their heels at passing along heirlooms is easy. They are afraid of losing something of themselves. Many people have certain items among their belongings that furnish them with a sense of connectedness, relevance, and comfort. It may be a vanity set, jewelry box, souvenir, photograph, or book. The "vital few" concept is a good philosophy to keep in mind when deciding which of your belongings you want to keep. When my ninety-five-year-old father decided on his own to move into a nursing home, he took his favorite worn green chair, his dog-eared Bible, and a photograph of my mother. He also brought along a deck of cards for playing solitaire, a book of crossword puzzles, and several large-print books of favorite poems and short stories. After deciding on these "vital few" items, it was easier for him to leave the rest of his personal effects.

The significance of cherished possessions is most evident when relocating to smaller quarters or moving to a long-term-care facility. Learning how to adjust to what's missing becomes a challenge. A feeling of "de-selfing" occurs, no matter how much you realize that possessions do not actually make up who you are. Sometimes the heart and mind don't connect, especially if an object had significant value to someone you love.

When Dad was moving out of his home after sixty-five years, one of his biggest concerns about leaving was, "What will happen to all my things?" He felt relieved when we said we would take his belongings to Texas after his house was sold. And, after moving Dad's furnishings from Kentucky to Houston, we brought him for a visit. He smiled with great pleasure as he slowly wandered around our home, seeing his possessions integrated into our family life. He sat on the old piano bench and played a few chords, even though he could no longer hear the music. Tenderly touching a marble-top table in our entry hall, Dad said, "Did you know your mother had the sales slip for this old table somewhere among her papers? It was dated 1798, I think. Amazing that it's still in good condition. Looks like it belongs right here." I told him I found that bill of sale and it is among my special papers.

One of my "vital few" items that I keep on a shelf is a small white china pitcher with now faded images of a little girl having a tea party with her dolls. That little pitcher brings back so many childhood memories that I have a difficult time parting with it. And would you believe, the spout is broken, just a little bit. But I still cherish it, perhaps even more because I remember being five when I broke it. That little container is not on my giveaway list. Someday it will disappear because it would have no meaning or value to anyone else. But for now, it sits on my shelf and pleases me when I use it to water my kitchen ivy.

Another of my cherished possessions is a stained-glass window that hung in the little Presbyterian Church in Newport, Kentucky, where I grew up. As a little kid, I used to sit in Sunday school class and look up at the beautiful arched window and feel a closeness to God. Our daughter, Susan, and her husband, Tom, admired the window and asked about its history. I told them that thirty years ago, when the old church was being sold, we bought the window and had it shipped to Houston.

Hearing their interest in this one-hundred-year-old art piece made me realize that they should have it and that this was the time to give it to them. It now hangs in their home and connects them to a long legacy of church heritage.

When you feel confident of *whom* you want to receive a particular treasure, and are comfortable that the *when* is now—that's the right time to give it away. So do it with great pleasure as often as you can. Then don't be surprised when most of your gifting experiences are absolutely wonderful. You will probably start looking for ways to make your cherished possessions giveaway list longer and longer, increasing the joy of naming special people to receive your precious things.

HOW TO DISTRIBUTE
YOUR CHERISHED POSSESSIONS

There is no one best way to pass on your cherished possessions—except the way that works best for you. In the next few pages, you'll find some random ideas, stories, and experiences. Perhaps one or more of them will inspire you to make some very important presentations to some very important people in your life.

The Presentation: The manner in which you pass on your possessions can add to the pleasure for both parties . . . and to the memories. So instead of just handing a gift to someone, make a presentation! In person! The idea is to make an event of it . . . an opportunity to give significance to your valued items and enhance your relationship with a much-loved family member or friend. There's a wide range of possibilities for how to do it. A special lunch or dinner can be the setting. Giftwrapping adds to the surprise (even if the receiver knows what it is). If it's too big to wrap, a big bow adds to the festivities.

Several years ago, I collected special things that I thought our daughter Toby would enjoy. Most of them were among my mother's cherished possessions. Included were a huge antique turkey platter, a brown crockery Bundt pan with ruffled sides, a set of six silver spoons, a monogrammed linen tablecloth with napkins, and a creamy yellow pottery pitcher.

When I gave these things to Toby, we sat at her kitchen table and had tea while I told her the story of each item. It was a wonderfully satisfying time for both of us, and she mentioned that she felt Gramma Little—my mother—was sitting with us. Remember, you are passing on a part of you and your heritage and creating memories that will live on.

Our son Rick has had his eye on our old walnut rocking chair with a deep carving on the back depicting a fat, jolly monk wearing a long robe and stirring a vat of wine. We have told Rick the monk is ready to live with him in Austin, and when we deliver it, we will drink a toast to the monk and his new home.

Of course, there are times when the most effective presentation is not dramatic. Quietly handing a gift to someone under certain circumstances may be the most meaningful and memorable thing you can do. And there may be times when anonymous giving will be the only appropriate presentation.

Ten-Best-Things List: A few years ago, Jenks and I wrote letters to our four kids asking them to name, in order of personal preference, "ten things in our home that you would like to have some day." That "Ten-Best-Things" letter has become an amusing epistle in the family. Our children walked through our home at different times, made notes, and listed what they liked. Now they tell us they want to redo their lists, because they have changed their minds or they see we have acquired some new cherished possessions. If we choose, we can give them some of these things while we are still alive. For now our file records which child will get various items, and they all know they can revise their list anytime. The family is pleased with the way we are handling this process.

Sometimes children are reluctant to say what items they would like to have because they don't want to think about their parents dying, or they are afraid they will appear greedy. Find ways to encourage family members to let you know what things are important to them. Otherwise you may miss opportunities or cause unnecessary disappointments.

Equal Treatment: Of course there is always the problem of how to keep everything equal among children and grandchildren. Most people struggle with this quandary. Keeping things even is a concern before you die, and it'll be a concern for others after you die if you have not previously distributed your cherished possessions. Being perceived as acting fairly is never an easy task. In fact, it is impossible. What may feel "equal" to you may not appear that way to others. It reminds me of Christmas when our kids were small. We always hoped to keep them happy by treating them all the same. Did you go through that quagmire? It was perplexing then and it still is. But you didn't stop giving gifts at Christmas. Nor should you hold back from passing along things now for fear of not doing it right. At least now you are able to explain your choices.

Waiting to do anything until you can do it perfectly translates into doing nothing. What if you waited to go to school until you knew for sure you would make straight As or waited to get married until you knew for sure you would be the perfect wife or husband or waited to have children until you knew for sure . . .

Labeling Cherished Possessions: If you have a preference about giving a special item to a particular person, but you are not ready to part with it, it is helpful to put some kind of label on the item. For example, leave a note inside a drawer or attached to the object, stating whom you want to enjoy that particular article. My mother put notes inside a teapot and in a vase naming our daughters as the ones to receive them.

A note tucked inside a drawer in Mother's desk told its history. "This cherry desk, with handblown glass panels in the cabinet doors above the writing area, is the oldest and most valuable piece of furniture we own. It was made for my Grandfather Weaver, Justice of the Peace in Weaversville, Pennsylvania, in the early 1800s. The six-foot side panels are made from one piece of wood. I want Margie to have it." This desk is where I had my daily devotions and read my Bible. Her handwritten explanation links me to my heritage. I love this antique, but it was not passed on to me until Dad moved to a nursing home. It is now among my cherished possessions, and I would not part with it for any amount of money. It will be among my special belongings until I have to move on. But it's already on our daughter Toby's "Ten-Best-Things" list.

The "Grab": In one family, the story goes, their mother and father left no instructions, so the fair-minded heirs held a "grab." It worked something like this: When the last parent died, the three daughters gathered at their childhood home, each with a roll of different colored tape. The first day the girls walked into a room and drew straws to decide who would pick first. Then they took turns, each one choosing items and marking them with her own color of tape. The next day they moved to a different room and followed the same procedure. They walked in the garden, attic, and the basement. When everything had been chosen, negotiations began in which trades were made, sometimes involving a combination of items. When the process ended, three moving vans arrived. The blue taped items went into one van, the red into another, and the yellow into the third van. The grab was over.

This plan, obviously, is an example of dividing cherished possessions after someone's death. But if you can't figure out how to apportion your belongings fairly among your heirs when you move into a nursing home or go to live with one of your children, you might suggest a grab as an option.

Giving Cherished Possessions for Special Occasions: Another way to give away your cherished possessions is to use special days—birthdays, anniversaries, birth of a baby, Christmas, Valentine's Day—to remember particular people with specific gifts. When our son Bob turned twenty-one, his grandfather (my dad) gave him a gold pocket watch that had been given to him when he was twenty-one. Bob bought a glass case to display it on his fireplace mantel.

For our daughter Susan's tenth birthday, we gave her a favorite framed drawing of a plump little girl that had hung in Jenks's home when he was a boy. The words under the picture make us smile: "Does anyone know of an ice cream soda that wants a good home?" And for Christmas this year, we gave our Santa Claus mugs to our two daughters. Any occasion can be the right time to transfer your cherished possessions to someone you choose.

Sell Your Possessions and Divide the Cash: Cash is certainly easier to divide. Some people believe dollars are more important than possessions. Before selling things, ask your heirs how they feel about your belongings. But if converting your possessions into currency is the method you want to use, go for it.

Estate Sale: Hattie sold her belongings at an estate sale before going to live in an assisted living facility. Two of her grandchildren attended and excitedly purchased a teapot and a picture. It's fun, and sometimes surprising, to discover the value of items that you own.

Garage Sale: After family members have made their choices, some people dispose of everything else at a garage sale or have a "giveaway party." They invite friends to take what they want. After the death of both parents, one family divided the most cherished possessions. They put a value on each of the remaining items, and by playing monopoly, they used make-believe money to purchase them.

Charities: When there are no heirs, decisions about possessions can become even more baffling. But you always have choices. Giving a part or all of your estate to benefit society is a way to leave the world a better place. A favorite professor in my graduate school lived alone in a modest home. When she died, she left a surprisingly large sum of money to provide scholarships at the school. Another childless couple has made the Salvation Army the sole beneficiary of their estate. Many people bequeath a part or all of their estate to their church.

If You Do Nothing: Remember, all good gifts come from God. Be a responsible steward of your blessings and your belongings. You always have the option to do nothing and let someone else make the decisions, but you will miss the joy of giving. It may relieve you of making difficult decisions, but, without instructions about your wishes, results rarely turn out the way you hoped.

The decisions may seem more difficult than they really are, however. Approach them in small steps, like picking out which items mean the most to you and writing out why they are special. The "Distribution of My Cherished Possessions" form at the end of this chapter can help get you started on this loving project. Whatever you do, label a folder in your Going-Away File "Cherished Possessions" and keep your most up-to-date list in this folder.

MY MOTHER'S FINAL GIFT

On Easter morning in 1967, I called my ninety-year-old mother in Kentucky to wish her Happy Easter. We were living in Kansas City then and had to watch our pennies. I was splurging a bit with a long-distance call. As soon as Mom answered the phone, she quickly told me, "Wait a minute, Margie. I have some things I want to *show* you."

Her choice of words surprised me. While waiting for her return, I became anxious, knowing my phone meter was running.

After what seemed like an eon of silence, Mom came back on the line and proceeded to tell me stories about antique items she had kept in a box. She described a small, black, folding parasol that had belonged to her grandmother. Her description of a beaded vest was so vivid I could visualize her mother wearing it to a special church function. Elbow-length lace gloves were part of the contents along with a black velvet purse and a straw sewing basket full of colored darning yarn. A long white christening gown and a small, child-sized, green pleated dress were described with loving words. She mentioned a homemade quilt with a red tulip design and a handwoven bedspread with the date 1821 embroidered in one corner. A book recording her father's sermons (he was a Lutheran minister) was included in the box. These treasures were unfamiliar to me. We ended our phone visit with, "I love you and God bless you."

The next day my mother died.

When I got home to Kentucky, Dad showed me a box on the floor near the telephone marked "Antiques for Margie." He said, "I don't know anything about these things, but your mother put them here by the phone while she was talking to you yesterday."

"Guess this is my inheritance," I said. Dad nodded. "Your mother left you much more than what's in that box, like her love of beauty, her trust in God, and the ability to be a good mother."

With awe and wonderment, I sorted through my new cherished possessions. Did Mother know she was going to die? I don't know. But I do know it was important for her to share her memories and stories with me while she was still here, and her treasures became an invaluable gift to my heart.

Distribution of My Cherished Possessions

My Cherished Items & Their Stories or Histories	My Plan for Them
1.	1.
2.	2.
3.	3.
4.	4.
5.	5.
6.	6.

*Signature*_____

*Date*_____

7

Writing Your Ultimate Bio

A UNIQUE WRITING OPPORTUNITY

Wouldn't it be wonderful if, when your time comes, virtually all plans were already made by the one person in the world most qualified to make them—you.

Writing your life's story is a good place to begin because it is a reminder of your own importance, remembering who you are, what you have enjoyed, and what you have achieved in this life.

Creating your own one-of-a-kind obituary is a unique writing opportunity in this final planning process. You can write it yourself or, if you like, have someone help you. You can also designate someone ahead of time to write your obituary then talk with him or her about what you would like it to say about you. If you write your own obituary and think of it as your ultimate bio, you'll be free to be more creative than someone else. And this can significantly add to the conversational therapy for your survivors. You can include humor and special-interest stories. Some obituaries poke good-natured fun at the deceased. This is especially touching if the reader knows you are talking about yourself.

I saw one notice that read "In lieu of flowers, have yourself a big heavenly dessert." Another stated "I avoided the infirmities of old age by eating what I liked, doing what I wanted, and rigorously refraining from all forms of bodily exertion." Some accounts take up several columns, like the detailed sketch in my hometown paper, describing the deceased as being well known among the police, and having served three jail terms. "Only one, the deceased admitted to."

In addition to briefly highlighting your life's story and accomplishments and providing some family background, this notice will announce the time and place of the funeral or memorial and burial service. (Of course, you will have to leave these last details for someone else to write.) It will also provide information about visitation, flowers, and charities. Some friends may want to put their personal closure on your life by honoring you with a contribution to a charity. Or if you, like some I know, feel that it is an imposition to suggest charities, just omit this item.

If you don't prepare your obituary in advance, funeral homes will do it and charge for this service. Or a family member can write the notice and hand-deliver it to the paper, but you will miss out on the pleasure of reminiscing in writing about your life, loved ones, and friends. You also will have little influence on what is ultimately said about you.

REMEMBERING YOUR LIFE

After rereading the published account of my mother's death, Dad suggested we think about what to say in his obituary. "I don't want a picture with it. They're doing a lot of that now. I want the write-up to be short and simple. But I would like it to mention that I was an exchange teacher in Beirut, Syria, from 1910 to 1913. I taught English and basketball. I'm proud of that experience. I was born May 10, 1884, in Oregon, Illinois. I became a history teacher and the principal at Newport High School. I don't want a casket in the memorial service or viewing of the body. Just invite folks to come to a memorial service, stay afterward, and have a good time. Do I need to include anything else?"

As Dad and I wrote his obituary, we relived his life. He told me stories about his childhood, his adventures in college, how he met Mom, and some of his life's disappointments. He talked about his belief in God and how he almost became a minister, but decided he could best use his God-given talents as a teacher. He was silent for a moment, then said, "You know, I think I have been ministering most of my life—in all the interactions I've had with students, the church, and you kids. I have a great faith that we can make it through anything that happens to us. I have tried to be fair and honest in all my dealings with people. And I wanted to make a difference in the world."

Hearing my father "talk out" what he wanted in his obituary was profoundly comforting to me, and it still is every time I remember those moments. I also sensed it was just as meaningful to him. I've forgotten much of what we put in the obituary, but the emotions, the awareness of the connection between Dad and me, the depth of love that I felt in this experience will always be with me, just because he asked me to help prepare his obituary.

Obituaries are not only important for the family; they also serve as a vital part of letting go for friends, neighbors, and other significant relationships. They are a reminder of who you are and can help others begin the process of healing. For all of the people in your life, talking about you is a very important part of the closure process. A good obituary generates and enhances many conversations that can calm the hearts of those left behind. Healthy grieving often includes talking and crying together about the person who is gone.

On the obituary page of any newspaper, you will see a wide

variety of notices. One of my favorites included a picture of a clown. Jako, a clown magician, died after dedicating seventeen years to doing a clown ministry in hospitals, where he brought joy, laughter, and encouragement to children and adults. Bodacious living was his life gift to others.

Another notice stated that the deceased did not need to name his survivors and friends. "They know who they are." One woman who died at the age of 114 "was the daughter of former slaves and was last seen picking tomatoes in her garden." Another grandmother died requesting "no service be held but everybody join together for a big barbecue celebration in the backyard."

Newspaper obituaries are intriguing. Reading them can provide clever ideas for writing your own. One way to begin the obituary process is to collect death notices that are interesting to you. But don't be limited by them. Be a little lavish with your prose. As time passes, while you are still alive, you can make additions or revisions.

It is important to be familiar with the logistics—like the cost per line of an obituary, which varies with the circulation of the newspaper. For instance, in 2002, the cost at the *Houston Chronicle* is $8.57 per line. A typical photo would add $135. In contrast, some small newspapers print brief death notices for no charge. Also, some newspapers only accept an obituary that is submitted through a local funeral home. Check with your paper to verify their requirements and current prices.

There are other publications that may need to be notified as well, and your survivors probably will be unaware of them. Make a record of any newspapers, organizations, school alumni newsletters, or businesses that should be informed. More people than you ever realized are interested in you. Other uses of the obituary might be including it in the funeral program or having it read at the service. It can be sent to family and friends who cannot attend the service.

An obituary also provides an excellent entry to be included in genealogy records. Use the following form to help guide your write-up. When you are satisfied with your creative work, put it in your Going-Away File under "Obituary."

Obituary Preparation Form

Full name and address _____

Date of birth _____

Place of birth _____

Parents' full names _____

Personal information

    Education _____

    Employment _____

    Fraternal organizations _____

    Honors/recognition _____

    Public service _____

    Special achievements _____

    Military service _____

Marital status (circle one)

Single   Married   Widowed   Divorced

Name of spouse (indicate if deceased) _____

Wedding date _____

Names of children and cities of residence _____

Names of grandchildren _____

Sisters and brothers (city and state of residence) _____

Memorials/charities _____

Picture (circle one)   Yes   No

Place of viewing, service, interment _____

Where to publish obituary:

    Newspapers _____
    Businesses _____
    Alumni publications _____

Write the most colorful story of your life you can. Fill in all the details and put this information in your Going-Away File under "Obituary."

8

FUNERAL HOME SELECTION

Until Mother's death, I had not planned a funeral. My older sister was unable to participate in the planning, and both of my brothers had already died away from home. Because Dad was stone deaf, he asked Jenks and me to make the arrangements. We walked into a funeral home in a small Kentucky town to begin the process. It never occurred to us to compare prices at another establishment.

In a typical "funeral voice," the mortician offered his condolences and then asked how we planned to honor "dearly beloved Mother." He was trying to help, but his false tone of bereavement turned me off. Mom and Dad had talked to me in some detail about what they wanted in their funerals. A plain pine box was their idea of a final resting place. When I expressed that choice, the funeral director's voice dropped an octave in deep concern. "How would dear Mother feel about your burying her in such a plain coffin? What will the neighbors think?"

I told him Mother would be pleased that we followed her instructions and the neighbors would understand.

Then ignoring all I had just said, he escorted us through several beautifully appointed rooms filled with elegant caskets. Again I mentioned my mother's request. In a sad voice, our guide explained, "Well, they are in the basement."

After we chose an inexpensive coffin, the mortician asked about purchasing "an appropriate shroud for dear Mother." I explained that Mom wanted an immediate burial and had already chosen her "going-away outfit." (Since Mom's death, funeral journal ads—and ways of spending money on a funeral—have expanded. A magazine, Practical Burial Footwear, is now advertising a "Fit-a-Fut-Oxford." It is designed to fit the deceased foot after rigor mortis sets in. Fortunately, we didn't have to make a decision about burial footwear in 1967.)

A limo was offered to carry our family to the church for the memorial service and to the cemetery afterward. Funeral home thank-you notes were suggested. And if we would provide necessary information, the funeral home would arrange to put the obituary in the newspaper. They thought of everything that was helpful . . . and expensive. I told him we would handle those details. Our do-it-yourself approach for Mom's funeral was definitely below the average cost.

When we told Dad about our funeral home experience, he expressed concern that they wouldn't want to have anything to do with him when he dies, after dealing with me. But he nodded in agreement, "You did the right thing."

Although we did not comparison shop funeral homes, we were fortunately able to get the services we wanted at a price with which we were comfortable. Choosing a funeral home without checking into costs, services, etc., can create an unexpected financial burden on the survivors. Most funeral homes provide sensitive, friendly, and valuable services. Some, however, are so profit-motivated that their sales techniques can easily influence survivors to make unwise and costly decisions. Keep looking until you find the one that feels right to you and whose financial arrangements are straightforward and understandable.

The aim of this chapter is to acquaint you with your options and sources of information so you can avoid intimidation, choose wisely, and select the one funeral home that you feel will provide the kind of funeral you desire. And to encourage you to make as many of those decisions as you can ahead of time.

Before a mortuary can tell you what their fees will be, they must know what services you want. So before talking to them, you should think through what kind of funeral would please you. There are basically three types of funerals: (1) Maximum Service: The funeral home provides elaborate assistance. (2) Moderate Service: The funeral home services are limited and the family performs some of the functions. (3) Minimum Service: The funeral home is involved very little. In the process of singling out, in advance, the services you want from a funeral home, you will help your survivors avoid paying charges that are not needed.

MORTUARY ADMINISTRATIVE FEE AND "OTHER CHARGES"

Most mortuaries have an administrative charge that goes into effect when they are called to pick up the body after a death. This fee may also be called a "General Service Charge" or a "Non-declinable Charge." This expense covers overhead, staff, and facilities. Some death care establishments have what they call a "basic service charge package" that includes picking up the body, use of their facility, and preparation of the body for burial. Since the list of charges for each funeral home is different, it is wise to explore what services their administrative charge includes.

Recently, a friend died in the hospital, and they asked her husband what funeral home to call to pick up her body. He gave them the name of a mortuary located near his home. He had never visited it but passed by the beautiful newly built structure on his way to work every day; it was just the first name that came to mind. The next day when he went to the funeral home to discuss the services he wanted, he told them all he needed was to have the body cremated and that a memorial service would be held in his place of worship. He would not need any other assistance. He was shocked to learn that their "administrative charge" of $5,000 began when the body was picked up. To change to another funeral home at that point would have been embarrassing and added more cost. He told me, "I see now the big advantage of making decisions ahead of time and knowing what the administrative charge includes."

The funeral home involvement is limited when cremation, immediate burial, or delivery of the body to an airport or train station for long-distance transportation is requested. In these cases, it would be critical to have a clear understanding about the administrative fee before asking a funeral home to pick up the body at the place of death.

When a mortician offers suggestions such as holding the service in the mortuary, providing a shroud, or a procession to the cemetery, it's easy to assume that all of those things are included in the general service fee when, actually, they are usually extra expense items. And some people don't realize that cemetery costs are also separate from funeral home charges. Cosmetic touch-up is also available so the deceased doesn't look so dead. Years ago, when Dad was ninety-seven, he and I attended a visitation of an old friend at the funeral home. We stood over the casket gazing down at the corpse. My deaf father announced in his booming voice, "Elsie never looked so good."

BURYING MONEY IN THE GROUND

As a rule it is the survivors who end up selecting a funeral home—making rushed decisions with crumpled hearts and clouded minds, right after the death of a loved one. And just before having to plan a memorial service and burial.

What more *unfavorable* conditions could there be for making sensitive and cost-efficient judgments? Survivors seldom have the presence of mind to even pray about such choices, much less ask advice and compare costs. Amid these circumstances a lot of money is buried in the ground—needlessly.

If you know what kind of funeral you want and discuss your plans with your family, you will have a much clearer picture of what mortuary to choose and the cost involved. But unless this subject is discussed beforehand, the typical funeral reflects survivors' hasty choices rather than the deceased's wishes. And many times, a costly funeral service is planned out of guilt or a lack of knowledge of the options or is a result of quick decisions—like throwing darts at the funeral section in the phone book.

A profusion of data about births, weddings, and college choices is easily available. Zillions of displays and books on these events fill the stores. Marketplaces hold special promotions to help new parents, brides, and students view options for these coming adventures. Customers who are making these choices research costs, quality, services, surroundings, and personnel at various establishments before making decisions. It is time for people to become just as free to take charge of their death adventure, and think and plan for all that is involved. You didn't have much say about how you came into this world, but you can have a lot to do with how you leave.

You want a mortuary that will provide quality service you can depend on at the price with which you are comfortable. Most funeral homes provide similar services. The determining factors are *price* and *integrity.*Choosing a funeral home close to you is important only if it provides integrity and the price you want. Location rarely should be the key to your selection. But it is all a matter of personal choice and of your commitment to make these important decisions now.

MAXIMUM FUNERAL SERVICE

A maximum funeral service means different things to different people. For example, a lot depends on the size of your community. In Houston, Texas, would probably be more elaborate than a funeral in Southgate, Kentucky. It also involves differences in local cultures. A full-service funeral in San Francisco or New Orleans is likely to be more flamboyant than one in another city. Religion and ethnicity illustrate other differences, but there are some generalities that are fairly common to all maximum funeral services.

A high-profile mortuary usually is engaged for a maximum funeral service plan. Such an establishment is apt to be located in a high rent area of town, might contain a flower shop, and has facilities for holding large attendance services within its building. It owns or has access to a number of limousines or other special vehicles used to pick up the body, transport the family to the service, and carry flowers in a police-escorted procession to a cemetery.

Body preparation and preservation services include storage, refrigeration, embalming, bathing, dressing, hair care, cosmetology, and other special care to ready the deceased for viewing at the funeral home or elsewhere. Most mortuaries can coordinate the purchase of a burial shroud (a loose-fitting cloth), cemetery lot, grave liner, tombstone, and inscription.

An expensive copper, satin lined casket may cost over $20,000. The funeral home can hire pallbearers to carry the casket in and out of a service, and provide personnel to serve as greeters at the visitation and funeral ceremony. A full-service funeral might include professional musicians and a catered meal after the ceremony.

One outdoor funeral service in California was an all-day ceremony that had been planned by the deceased during the last years of her life. It started out at ten-thirty in the morning with her husband reading a special greeting from his deceased wife. Her children were involved lighting candles, playing bagpipes, and reading poems. An intermission lunch was served, and the service ended with a grief ritual, storytellers, a professional dance performance, and a graveside service, followed by a dinner and dance in a nearby country club.

A maximum service funeral can be as elaborate as you wish. Many people feel that their funeral is their last chance to make a statement about themselves. A last hurrah! Some enjoy the splendor of an imposing monument to mark the grave site. On strolls through Evergreen Cemetery in Southgate, Kentucky, we have been awed with the regal tombstones that mark many family plots. If that is what you want, go for it, enjoy planning it yourself, and let your loved ones in on your strategy. But keep the cost of your production in mind, and arrange to cover the expenses so your survivors will not be financially burdened trying to fulfill your wishes.

MODERATE FUNERAL SERVICE

Choosing a moderate funeral service indicates fewer services performed by a less pricey mortuary. A moderately priced quality casket might cost between two and five thousand dollars. And if you don't want it to be present in the memorial service, a less expensive wooden casket will be okay. If cremation is your preference, no casket is needed, and an urn could be buried in a cemetery, placed in a mausoleum or columbarium, or scattered at a place of your choice. A service may be held at a church or location other than the funeral home. Family and friends can handle some of the services, such as writing the obituary and acting as hostesses at the service, and family cars may be used instead of hiring limousines.

If immediate burial is your choice, the body, with minimum preparation cost, will be buried promptly after death. All of the expenses of a formal procession to the cemetery are eliminated. A less elaborate reception may be held after the service. The family can provide a signature book for people to sign at the service, and personal thank-you notes can be used rather than the ones offered by the funeral home.

It is necessary to know all the options you have to choose from before making your decision. The amount of money you have available to pay for your funeral service will influence your choices. At a recent conference of funeral directors, it was estimated that the average funeral in the United States costs between $5,000 and $8,000, which does not include burial charges.

MINIMUM FUNERAL SERVICE

A minimum funeral service will require less assistance from the mortuary. A less expensive casket can be purchased for around $500. A simple graveside service can be held with only the family and friends participating, or an informal memorial service can be held in a church or a public park with no reception afterward. A low-cost grave marker can be installed with minimum expense.

Immediate burial definitely reduces the total cost of a funeral, although that may not be the only reason for exercising this option. With that choice, the only mortuary services needed will be transporting the deceased (from the place of death to the funeral home and then to the cemetery) and minimal preparation of the body. A low-cost casket can be used if you choose to have a modest service in a church or at home.

I heard about one immediate burial in which family and friends gathered at a private home after the funeral. Special prayers were offered and memories of the deceased were shared. Afterward they snacked on wine and cheese.

Immediate burial may be delayed because of the time needed to get a signed death certificate, or if the burial site or mausoleum space is not immediately available. In those situations, the body may be stored or refrigerated until the grave site is ready. Embalming would be required only if the body is to be stored for a long period of time or transported to a distant location.

When only minimal services are desired, it is very important to arrange with the funeral home ahead of time to preclude the normal administrative fee. You will have little or no use for the high overhead cost of a pricey mortuary establishment. Also, your burial arrangements will make a difference in the total funeral charges.

FUNERAL CONSUMERS ALLIANCE

Funeral Consumers Alliance is also known in some states as "Funeral and Memorial Societies." They provide information about funeral-planning societies in nearly every state in the country. They will aid you in your funeral home selection and can save you money. For membership information and guidance, they can be reached on the Internet at www.funerals.org.

We have benefited from our membership in the Houston chapter. Mailings explain legislation and law changes. Speakers from the funeral profession as well as other informed people report at our annual chapter meetings on what is happening in the area of funeral planning. Members often recount their personal experiences, providing valuable insight into the mortuary business.

Local chapters of Funeral Consumers Alliance contract with selected mortuaries for modest cost funeral or crematory services for its members. This organization promotes dignity, simplicity, and economy in funerals and memorial services. The society sends new members a packet of funeral information and forms to aid in the decision making.

SHOP BEFORE YOU DROP

Most people don't realize that they have the right to comparison shop funeral home prices, just like you would shop for a suit or a dress. You can pay a high price or a reasonable price for basically the same service. What you *want* and can *afford* are the deciding factors. The best way to handle the selection process is to know the price before you buy. So you shop before you drop—gathering information by phone or personal visits about the alternatives.

The "Funeral Services Cost Survey" and the form labeled "My Choice of Funeral Home and Services" at the end of chapter 9 are designed to help you in your selection process. Because funeral home services and burial services often overlap, the evaluation forms for both are at the end of the next chapter on Grave Matters. Funeral home price lists are public information, but you have to request it. Any hesitancy on the part of a funeral home is reason enough to delete that one from your list. Also at the end of this chapter, you will find a listing of items to help you select your funeral home. And, of course, you will want to put all of this information in your Going-Away File.

The image that most often comes to mind when thinking of a bereaved family rushing to get ready for the funeral of a loved one (I bet you're seeing it in your mind now) is this: a family member or two, attended by a solemn undertaker in a mortuary showroom, looking at caskets. Actually, since you have time now to shop and a casket is a major expense item, this should be one of the last costs you check out. There is no sense looking at caskets and getting deeply involved with a mortuary until your selection of a funeral home is narrowed down to one or two. And before you get casket prices from funeral homes, research a couple of those new businesses that specialize in direct sales of caskets. Or you can buy one on the Internet. Some shoppers even approach this idea with a bit of humor. Someone told me that visiting a casket warehouse was like going to "Kaskets 'R' Us," and one cartoon suggested you build your own coffin and use it for a coffee table until you need it.

Try to take someone with you when you visit funeral homes (as well as cemeteries and casket and monument companies). Having someone along will increase your comfort level (and self-confidence) and usually helps in making decisions. Without emotional support and rational input, most people don't take advantage of comparison shopping and needlessly bury a lot of money in the ground.

After all, your wishes are intended to make your death easier on the survivors, so try to talk to them now. People differ greatly in their comfort level and tolerance for conversing about life's final passage. For me, it was much easier to exchange views with Dad about the end of his life than it was to talk to Mom about her last chapter. Since money was scarce, being practical was the rule of the day for her. The high cost of dying worried her so much that she thought it was wasteful to send flowers to a funeral. Mom once told me, "A wedding is just like a funeral except that you get to smell your own flowers." At age ninety, she still valued beauty and appearance, but her love of flowers was in conflict with another reality of the times, limited resources.

Although it has been over thirty years since I planned Mom's funeral, I still have a deep sense of regret over how I handled one part of it. I followed her wishes: "Don't waste flowers on my funeral." I requested that, in lieu of flowers, contributions could be sent to her church or other charitable institutions in her honor. Her memorial service was held on a dreary day in a gloomy sanctuary . . . quite a contrast to my attractive, charming mother—a lover of beauty. And there was not a flower in that church. I wish I had been wiser and less practical. At the time of a death, people often do not make good decisions. Nor do they see all the alternatives. Flowers would have reflected Mom's spirit and celebrated her loveliness. Looking back and wishing I had done it differently is an example of the hidden cost of dying. I realize now that flowers at the time of a death are for the survivors and add beauty to the service.

Most survivors feel swamped with details, not to mention sadness. Mom's clear directions served as a useful guideline for me because I knew what she wanted. I carried out her wishes, but I didn't satisfy my own desire to celebrate her life.

It is important to add a P.S. at the end of your Going-Away Plan that in essence says something like: "My dear children, these are my wishes, but please know that you are free to adjust them in any way that will make my passage easier for you."

TO HELP YOU SELECT YOUR FUNERAL HOME

1. First, *commit* to selecting a funeral home.
2. Talk to the Funeral Consumers Alliance about information and brochures they offer, and consider membership. Call 1-800-765-0107.
3. Collect price lists and other information from several funeral homes, casket stores, cemeteries, and monument companies. Record your findings on the form "Funeral Services Cost Survey." Visit two or more mortuaries to narrow down your choices.

4. Discuss your ideas and findings with someone(s) you love and trust.
5. Select the mortuary that you feel would be best for your funeral.
6. Fill out the form "My Choice of Funeral Home at the end of the next chapters."
7. Put this information in your Going-Away File.

9

GRAVE MATTERS

When I was a little girl, Evergreen Cemetery was my playground. My best friend, Mattie Morgan, lived there. Her father was the gravedigger. We would jump down into a newly dug grave, stretch out on the bottom, hold hands, lie very still, and play dead. Then we'd giggle, scramble out, and run free. When a funeral cortege circled around the winding paths of the cemetery, it was like a parade. Because of my childhood experiences, cemeteries bring back pleasant memories. They can also provide comfort and resolution to many who visit their loved ones' burial sites.

This was not the case for my client Tessa, however. Throughout her life, she and her mother had many conflicts—and were never close. When this young woman came to my office she was angry and feeling helpless. "Now we can never work out our disagreements. Mom died before we settled our differences. Do I have to live the rest of my life feeling this way?"

Tessa's grievances dated back to childhood and later included her mother's lack of interest when her first baby was born. She felt criticized for everything, but she had never been able to discuss these things with her mother. Most of her mother's cherished possessions had been given away without asking Tessa if she was interested in keeping any of them. She had few happy memories of her mother, and now it was too late.

I asked what she wished she could have said to her mother. What would make it better for her now? After several sessions, I suggested she visit the cemetery, stand by her mother's grave, and talk about her feelings. "Maybe write a letter and read it at the grave site. Then think about your mother's life. Think about what she might say to you today, and what you want to understand."

She scoffed at the idea. How could that possibly help?

A few months later, Tessa came into my office with a smile on her face. "You won't believe this," she said, "but I went out to the cemetery, sat by Mother's grave, and talked about all my hurts. In my mind she heard me. And even answered me. I imagined that I could actually hear her explain what was behind all the criticism. Mom had a lot of pain in her life, but I had never listened to her problems. Now I have a better understanding of her behavior and feel a sense of peace between us."

This sense of peace was also what Hallie's children were seeking at the end of her life. Hallie had lived the last years of her life in great pain from stomach cancer and as a hostage to Alzheimer's disease. When she died at the age of eighty-seven, she was cremated, and her family arranged for a priest to accompany them out into the Gulf of Mexico where they scattered her ashes from the back of a boat as the priest prayed and released her to God. The children felt great relief and closure and a wonderful sense of letting go, knowing their mother had suffered for many years and was finally free.

There was a time when the only way I knew for taking care of grave matters was a simple burial in a cemetery. Cremation was so rare and was thought by many in my "Christian" community to be quite "un-Christian." I knew nothing about body donations, and not much more about mausoleums and columbariums. Today information about these other options gives you a much wider range of choices. If you have a preference for your burial, let your loved ones know now. With that selection already known at the time of your death, arrangements can be made without your survivors having to wonder about your wishes.

Although burials and funerals today have become big business, most people don't think much about what is involved until tragedy strikes, and they are forced to make emergency decisions. Consequently, too many choices are made without forethought and planning. And the problem takes on more complexity because of the wide range of body disposition options that are now available. It's like breakfast cereals: There used to be corn flakes and shredded wheat on the shelf in the grocery store. Now there are so many brands that I have to plan on five minutes in the cereal section searching for my favorite.

The choice you make for your burial can have a lasting effect on your survivors. The purpose of this chapter is to identify and define various burial choices and what is involved with each one, so you can make informed decisions. Four burial options are (1) earth, (2) mausoleum, (3) cremation, and (4) body donation. Your preference will determine the services that will be required of the funeral home you select.

EARTH BURIAL

The most common way of caring for the dead in this country has been earth burial in a cemetery. In years past, church property usually included a cemetery for its members. Some of these are still in use, especially in rural areas. Similarly, in the past, it was not unusual for families to maintain their own private graveyards. Many cemeteries these days, however, are owned by large for-profit corporations whose managers do not know the families of the deceased.

If you choose a conventional burial, the plot can be selected and paid for ahead of time. But situations could change that would alter the location or need for your burial plot. For example, you might move to a different part of the country or the person in charge of your burial could make another arrangement and not use the plot you paid for. But some people feel more comfortable if they pay for a burial place and enjoy knowing where they will be buried.

In 1993 my sister-in-law and her husband went a step further. At Evergreen Cemetery, they erected a grave marker with their names and dates of birth inscribed on it. All that is needed now is to add the year of death for each one. Fortunately, they did not have "19__" carved into the stone, since they both expected to live into this millennium.

To prevent the ground from sinking and to reduce maintenance, most cemeteries require either a grave liner made of concrete slabs assembled at the site or a coffin vault, which is a one-piece unit with a top usually made of concrete or fiberglass. A grave liner is about half the price of a concrete vault. Either type is satisfactory, and they can be bought at the same time and place as the casket, or can be purchased from a separate vendor.

Remember that your choice of plot can bring a lot of comfort to your survivors. In 1967, after Mother's death, Dad and I visited the cemetery where he had paid two hundred dollars for six plots. "You were about six when I bought these, and the Great Depression had already started. Your mother and I thought we made a good deal here at Forest Lawn, and we wanted to be ready when our time came. Two hundred dollars was a lot of money back then, and now it turns out that none of you four kids will use these lots. Your Aunt Ora and Uncle Billy are buried here along with Uncle Ernie. We used one plot to mark the deaths of your brothers even though there are no bodies in that grave. (John's body was never recovered when his plane went down in the South Pacific during the war in 1943. Bob died in 1970 after retiring from the Air Force; he was cremated and his ashes scattered off the coast of California.)

My father really loved the spot he had picked. "I'm glad we have this place. There are no headstones or monuments here, just bronze plaques on the ground. There are no fake flowers or whirligigs on the graves." A "perpetual care" charge had been included when they bought the graves, which covered the cost of caring for the grave site; the staff maintains it well. Some people have donated benches in memory of loved ones so that it looks a bit like a park. "When I stand here on my plot, next to your mother's grave," he said, "I like the view. Ducks in the pond near a weeping willow tree. This will be a good place for me."

We sat together on a nearby bench. He put his hand on my knee. "I like these plain grave markers that are flat on the ground. Nothing fancy. But I remember from my childhood that some tombstones had very interesting inscriptions. There was one that read 'She always said her feet were killing her, but nobody believed her.'" Then Dad said, "Did you hear about the graveside service where the clergyman stepped too close and fell in. He yelled out, 'Will someone help resurrect me?'"

I told him the old story about two gravediggers that stood at a distance from a newly dug grave . . . watching. A woman had requested burial in her red Cadillac. As the beautiful vehicle was lowered into the oversized tomb, one man commented, "Man, now that's really living."

MAUSOLEUM

Cemeteries also frequently offer above-ground burial in a mausoleum, which is usually a stone or marble structure with many spaces for the entombment of the dead in caskets or funeral urns. The most famous mausoleum was at Halicarnassus in southwest Turkey, built around 353–350 B.C. It held the remains of Mausolus, an ancient provincial ruler of the Persian Empire and is where the word *mausoleum* originated. This man-built structure of white marble was so huge, 135 feet high, and beautiful that it became one of the Seven Wonders of the World. Earthquakes have virtually destroyed this elaborate sepulcher. The Taj Mahal in Agra, India, is another well-known mausoleum.

Not all mausoleums are as famous. We have friends who have purchased two spaces in a mausoleum at Evergreen Cemetery in Southgate, Kentucky. Their names and birth dates are already inscribed on a brass plaque on the front. When they die, they want their bodies to be taken to the mausoleum for immediate burial without waiting for funeral rites. The family will hold a memorial service in their church with no casket present. Our friends feel a sense of satisfaction now that they have made arrangements and know how and where they will be buried.

CREMATION

Cremation is the process of reducing a body to ashes. Then the cremated remains (also called cremains) are shipped or hand-delivered to the family in a small container or an urn. It is advisable to request that the cremains be pulverized, especially if the family plans to scatter the ashes.

Cremation is becoming increasingly popular. Because of the scarcity of land, the simplicity of the procedure, and the lower cost, it is predicted that in the near future 50 percent of all deaths in the United States will involve cremation. In many parts of the world, it is a common way for disposing of the bodies of the deceased. But because the practice is relatively new to many people, it is often misunderstood.

One crematorium received a request for information and was asked, "Does the cost of cremation include the urinal?"

Unless the family chooses to hold a viewing of the body before cremation, a casket or embalming is usually not required. If a viewing is planned, a casket may be rented for the service before cremation takes place. The cremation cost survey form at the end of this chapter will help you evaluate this option.

While considering cremation as a choice, it will be helpful to talk with a funeral home or a crematory about the process, cost, and other implications. Then when you feel comfortable, discuss your decision with your family. If your choice for cremation draws strong objections from any member of your immediate family, some funeral homes will refuse to cremate.

A son asked his eighty-seven-year-old mother if she wanted to be buried or cremated. She thought about it for a minute, then said, "Surprise me."

There are many choices for dispersing cremated remains: burial, scattering, preservation in an urn by the family, or placement in a columbarium, an assembly of niches designed to hold small containers of cremains. Some churches have columbariums within the building or as part of a garden wall. The cost of buying a space in a columbarium is usually less than burial in the ground or a mausoleum.

Mausoleums also may have niches for cremains in small chambers, where a container of ashes might be visible through a glass panel, along with life symbols of the departed. I have seen such things as golf balls, a baseball glove, a pack of Lucky Strike cigarettes, a gold cross, pictures, a Bible, a prayer rug, a Star of David, and a rosary displayed in these windowed compartments.

Family members can scatter ashes in a private garden, or the Coast Guard can be contacted to spread them over the water. Cremains may be kept in an urn, or if you choose, the funeral home or crematory can dispose of the ashes. This alternative as opposed to cemetery burial can substantially lower the burial cost.

For those who want to go out with a bang, Pacific Memorial of Los Angeles will incorporate cremains into a fireworks display. I read that Congresswoman Pat Schroeder wants her ashes to be made into a doorstop, so she can hold doors open for people.

Death didn't stop LSD guru Timothy Leary and *Star Trek* creator Gene Roddenberry from hitching a ride into outer space in 1997. CNN reported that Leary's and Roddenberry's ashes, along with twenty-two other fans of space exploration, were on board when a Pegasus rocket launched from a Lockheed L-1011 jetliner over the Canary Islands. The main mission—a joint project between the University of California-Berkeley and a Spanish aerospace institute—was to launch Spain's first research satellite. But along for the ride were the cremated remains of individuals who had each paid $4,800 to become one with the universe. Packed in a canister with lipstick-sized vials, each containing seven grams of human ashes, they will orbit the Earth for six years before they reenter the atmosphere and burn up. This launch drew attention to the growing popularity of cremation, as well as the creative possibilities of going out in style.

My friend Jenny was on vacation with her husband in Norway when he died. After she discovered the exorbitant cost of shipping his body home, she decided on cremation. She brought his cremains home in her bag, then held a memorial service in their church.

BODY AND ORGAN DONATIONS

Body and organ donations are gifts of love. Donating your body, organs, or tissue to a medical school is a low-cost, high-benefit alternative. Organ procurement organizations provide a humane benefit by ethically, effectively, and efficiently recovering transplantable organs and tissues to give renewal of life to needy recipients. There is an unending demand for transplantable organs. A single donor can potentially help fifty patients. Erma Bombeck, one of America's favorite family writers, died while waiting for a liver transplant.

One of my clients, Gary, was luckier. He had been ill for a long time, waiting and wondering if he would live long enough to walk his daughter down the aisle. His only hope was in getting a transplant. After receiving a donor's kidney, not only was he there for his daughter's wedding but he now plays baseball with his grandson.

Universities, research hospitals, and eye banks are all in need of donors. According to the annual report by the United Network for Organ Sharing, transplant operations in the United States were up 44 percent from 1990 to 1999. Medical schools prefer an "enrolled donor," a person who has filed a bequest during his or her lifetime. For information about body donation, call a medical school in your state and ask about the "Willed Body Program." In her book *Caring for the Dead*[1], Lisa Carlson includes a complete list of medical schools in every state that accept body and organ donations, or call 1-800-765-0107.

It is essential that your family agree with your decision to donate organs or your body. If there is any objection by any family member, a medical school can refuse to accept the body. There is no remuneration for body donations, but some medical schools do pay for transportation of the body at the time of death. And most pay for final disposition.

Body donation can eliminate the cost of burial. As a safeguard, an alternative plan should be made for the disposition of the body, in case the willed body is rejected. Causes for body rejection may be contagious disease, recent surgery, autopsy, obesity, or family objection.

An elderly grandfather was urged by his family to talk about his last wishes. He refused. Said he did not like the options, and besides, he didn't want to be bothered. His daughter reminded him he could be cremated, but he said that where he was going would be hot enough. She suggested burial in the local cemetery, but he didn't like the idea of being covered with dirt. A son mentioned he could donate his body to science. Grandfather was not familiar with that choice and asked what was the purpose. His son explained that medical students used corpses for research, and to learn about the human body. The old man pondered the alternatives, and later announced, "I've decided to donate my body to science. My parents always wanted me to go to medical school."

IMMEDIATE BURIAL

In recent years immediate burial has gained increasing acceptance. In this practice, the body is picked up at the location of death and interred or cremated as quickly as possible before or without a funeral ritual. A memorial service may be held at the convenience of the family. Since the burial site or crematory may not be immediately available, storage and/or refrigeration of the body may be necessary at a funeral home. An inexpensive wooden coffin is all that is required for earth burial. Because there is minimal preparation of the body and less handling of the casket, immediate burial eliminates or reduces many costs. Of course, this arrangement is logical only if no viewing is planned and the casket is not to be present at the memorial service.

In October 1984 my one-hundred-year-old father died in his room at Carmel Manor Nursing Home before I got home to Kentucky. Since he and I had previously arranged for the immediate burial of his body and had informed the nursing home personnel, they knew what funeral home to call. His body was picked up and buried at Forest Lawn Cemetery in the plot he and I visited many times. Our family was able to concentrate on planning a memorial service that would honor him and celebrate his life.

COST SURVEY

At the end of this chapter you will find cost survey forms for the three body disposition options: earth burial, mausoleum, and cremation. You may use these forms to gather and record comparative costs from several funeral homes and cemeteries. This information will help you make better choices—whether you purchase these services before death, or simply gather information for your going-away plan that will help your survivors make quicker and wiser decisions.

The cost of cemetery lots has increased a great deal since Dad made his investment. Often grave plots and caskets can be purchased at significant savings from newspaper ads, many of which have been placed by people (or their survivors) who purchased plots and then, due to some change in circumstances, decided not to use them. They may be good buying opportunities, but keep in mind that instead of purchasing funeral services or burial lots in advance, other alternatives are available and usually are more satisfactory.

One final note: Be very cautious about prepaid burial and funeral services. The Consumers Unions' Southwest Regional office has warned, "Plain and simple, prepaid [funeral] contracts are not a fair deal for consumers. Almost any other long-term savings plan, including certificates of deposit, would generate enough interest to cover future inflation with money to spare." And with a prepaid plan, you stand to lose much of your investment if you move across the country or make some other significant change.

A wiser plan to take care of future funeral needs might be to set up a separate savings account or purchase an insurance policy to cover burial costs.

THE FIRST THING TO DO AFTER A DEATH

After a person dies, the first thing that must be done is to remove the deceased from the location of death. Most often a funeral home is called to transport the body to where it will be prepared for burial, cremation, viewing, or whatever the family has chosen. There may be exceptions when a body is donated and the receiving institution has its own transportation vehicle. In some situations, the city or county coroner may take over and remove the body.

After a mortuary picks up the body, they will store it by refrigeration or embalming, depending on what is appropriate for the services requested. Sometimes a grave site may take several days to prepare. Circumstances may delay burial, or it might be necessary to transport the body out of town to a family plot in another state. In that case, a family member usually accompanies the body on a plane or train.

A friend's parents retired in Florida. Before they died, they let their children know that they wanted to be buried in a church graveyard in Asheville, North Carolina. Arrangements were made with two funeral homes—one in Fort Myers and one in Asheville. Special savings had been put aside to cover the expense. One of the children accompanied the bodies on the plane to North Carolina, where a simple graveside service was held at the interment.

A client in my office told her daughter, Jyl, that she wanted to be buried in Israel where she was born. Jyl reminded her mother how expensive that would be to fly her body and a family member back to Israel. The mother said, "Well, you asked me what I wanted, so I told you. I know it would cost a lot. Make whatever arrangements you want. I can live with that." The mother laughed. "Guess I should say, I can die with that."

Grave matters are serious business, but the burden on survivors can be eased a great deal if you take responsibility for exploring options, making pertinent decisions before your death, and sharing this information with significant others. Preparing for life's final exit is many sided. What do you want as your ultimate resting place? Put this information in your Going-Away File in a file called "Burial Information."

GRAVE MATTERS TO CONSIDER

1. Evaluate burial choices:
    • Earth burial
    • Mausoleum
    • Cremation
    • Body donation
    • Immediate burial
2. Consider the cost of various options and how it will affect your choice for last rites.
3. Discuss your decision with your family.
4. Consider how your body will get to the burial site.
5. Prepare the following survey to help compare funeral services costs.

Funeral Services Cost Survey

Service	Funeral Home A	Funeral Home B	Funeral Home C
Administration fee	$ _____	$ _____	$ _____
Transport to funeral home	$ _____	$ _____	$ _____
Transport to other facility	$ _____	$ _____	$ _____
Transport of family to cemetery	$ _____	$ _____	$ _____
Transport of flowers to church	$ _____	$ _____	$ _____
Transport of flowers to cemetery	$ _____	$ _____	$ _____
Police escort	$ _____	$ _____	$ _____
Casket	$ _____	$ _____	$ _____
Vault or grave liner	$ _____	$ _____	$ _____
Body preparation:			
Refrigeration	$ _____	$ _____	$ _____
Bathing	$ _____	$ _____	$ _____
Hair	$ _____	$ _____	$ _____
Cosmetology	$ _____	$ _____	$ _____
Dressing	$ _____	$ _____	$ _____
Funeral service expenses:			
Visitation per day	$ _____	$ _____	$ _____
Chapel	$ _____	$ _____	$ _____
Memorial book/cards	$ _____	$ _____	$ _____
Death certificate	$ _____	$ _____	$ _____

Grave Matters

Service	Funeral Home A	Funeral Home B	Funeral Home C
Church service fee	$ _____	$ _____	$ _____
Grave site service fee	$ _____	$ _____	$ _____
Burial expenses:			
Opening/			
closing grave	$ _____	$ _____	$ _____
Mausoleum	$ _____	$ _____	$ _____
Marker	$ _____	$ _____	$ _____
Inscription	$ _____	$ _____	$ _____
Installation	$ _____	$ _____	$ _____
Cremation costs:			
Cremation	$ _____	$ _____	$ _____
Urn	$ _____	$ _____	$ _____
Scattering	$ _____	$ _____	$ _____
Earth burial	$ _____	$ _____	$ _____
Mausoleum	$ _____	$ _____	$ _____
Columbarium	$ _____	$ _____	$ _____
Marker	$ _____	$ _____	$ _____
Inscription	$ _____	$ _____	$ _____
Installation	$ _____	$ _____	$ _____
Grand total	$ _____	$ _____	$ _____

My Choice of Funeral Home and Services

Name_____ Date _____
Funeral home name _____
    Address _____
    Phone _____
    Contact person _____

Choice of Services	**Cost**
Funeral home administration fee	$ _____
Transportation of body:	
From place of death to funeral home	$ _____
To burial site	$ _____
To crematorium	$ _____
To other facility	$ _____
Other transportation:	
Flower car to cemetery	$ _____
Family to cemetery	$ _____
Police escort	$ _____

Casket   Yes   No $ _____
    Purchased from:_____
    Stock number/description _____

Cremation   Yes   No $ _____
Ashes   Yes   No $ _____
    Location: _____
Scattered   Yes   No $ _____
    Location: _____

Funeral service Yes   No $ _____
    Location: _____

Memorial Service Yes   No $ _____
    Location: _____

Visitation   Yes   No $ _____
    Location: _____

Grave site service:
         Yes   No $ _____
    Location: _____

Other requests: _____ $ _____

Grand total: _____ $ _____

10

YOUR GOING-AWAY PARTY

I read somewhere that Woody Allen said, "I don't mind dying. I just don't want to be there when it happens." But it is important "to be there" in the planning process. One of our church members told me, "We need better funerals. Too many are dismal and dreary. Why can't they be uplifting services that include lively music, heartwarming comments, humorous incidents, and shared happy memories of the person who died? A celebration of life."

What would "going out in style" mean to you? Whatever your answer, you can be the one in charge of making thoughtful plans and decisions, and letting your family (or some trusted friend) know what you want and where you keep your Going-Away File.

Wouldn't it be grand if your life's last ritual could be a special event, a salute to your life—a going-away party? You may not be able to formulate all the ingredients for an easy death, but there are many ways to leave this world, and you can let your loved ones know what kind of send-off would please you. Variety can be the spice of death.

You are well on your way if you have decided the method for your body disposition—burial, mausoleum, cremation, or body donation—and if you have selected your funeral home, along with the services you want. Now, the final step. It's time to plan the ceremony, if indeed you want a ceremony. This chapter assumes that you *do* want a going-away party and offers some ideas that might help you plan a really good one.

VISUALIZING YOUR MEMORIAL SERVICE

Before structuring everything in detail, I urge you to find a comfortable place where you can sit or lie down in a calm, peaceful atmosphere. Then let yourself imagine—both visually and verbally—those attending your service. Start with a prayer, asking God to guide you with ideas that would be uplifting and inspiring, as well as comforting and healing for your family and friends. What experiences would you want them to have? What kind of consoling affirmations would help them? After pondering these emotional issues, examine some of the practical decisions you will need to make.

Do I want . . .
- a service in the church?
- a service in a funeral home?
- a graveside service?
- an informal service?
- a reception?
- something else entirely?

Your responses to these questions will tell you how to look meaningfully at all the options that are available.

Do you want a more formal or informal service? Think about funeral services you have attended, the printed programs you've seen, the experiences you thought were most desirable . . . or most undesirable. What about those details you always wished "they" would include at funerals. Dad used to ask, "Why don't they tell some humorous stories at funerals and make the service more enjoyable?"

Following is a list of options to consider as you plan your own fully customized service. To provide a broad enough range of ideas to speak to the interests of a variety of readers, many items are listed here that you may not want to consider. As you go through the list, mark through everything you definitely would *not like* to include in your funeral service. That will leave your preferred list of options. Of course, you will think of some things that I do not mention.

OPTIONS TO CONSIDER: PRELIMINARY DECISIONS

Who to Inform When You Die: When I think about the time of my own death, among the first things I would like my family to do is call a limited number of people who should be informed immediately. Another list of folks could be called the next day after the time and place of the service have been established.

Figuring out whom to call could be a challenge. But, with a little preplanning on my part, this task will be greatly simplified. My personal address book in the kitchen desk drawer lists almost everyone I know. But I don't think they all would come to my memorial service. Like the plumber, the appliance service technician, or our house painter.

Then there's my appointment book with the tapestry cover. It has an address list in the back that might be a better place for my family to look for a list of names. It includes people I regularly contact, including my answering service. But it still would be much easier for my survivors, especially under the stress of the event, if I prepared a separate list with names and phone numbers, including my church and pastor, my primary doctor, my funeral home choice, my current clients, and others who should be called as soon as possible. Clergy should be notified immediately after your death, to comfort the survivors and assist in preparing the service and so that a notice can appear in the church bulletin or newsletter.

When you make your list, keep it brief. Your family will be going through enough without having to sit at the phone for hours. Suggest friends who could help with the calls.

Burial Clothing: One question a funeral director will ask is, "What clothes will the deceased wear at the time of burial?" Sometimes the burial garment is a shroud, a loose-fitting cloth or sheet that can be purchased from a funeral home, but you may prefer to be buried in your own clothes.

The decision about what you want to wear is, of course, influenced by your burial choice. If there is a viewing, this issue becomes more important. In addition to clothes, it could involve makeup, jewelry, glasses (on or off), and any other special items, such as a favorite hat, cane, purse, or military or fraternal insignia that you would like included. I remember when my Grampa was buried in 1928; he was wearing a dark suit with his gold G.A.R. (Grand Army of the Republic) badge worn proudly on his coat lapel along with his Spanish American War medal.

Do remember, however, that the funeral home needs to be informed about any of these items, especially jewelry that should be removed *before* burial. My mother was buried before I thought about removing her wedding ring. I felt sad about that, but I did not think it would be appropriate to have Mom exhumed just to retrieve the ring.

When our daughter Toby saw me wearing a new outfit, she exclaimed, "Oh, Mom, you look so great in that; maybe you'll want to be buried in it." Since I want to be cremated, however, I don't need a fancy dress to wear at the time of my death. My warmup clothes would be a lot more comfortable for my last journey.

If you care about what clothes are used for your burial, you should definitely let this be known. Too often, misunderstandings can happen with survivors, sometimes completely unintentionally. Rex dressed quickly when his father died very early in the morning. He grabbed his New York Yankees baseball jacket and cap and followed the funeral car that had picked up his dad's body. At the funeral home, he tossed his jacket and cap on a chair while making final arrangements. Hours later when leaving the mortuary, he forgot them. Upon returning to the funeral home for the viewing and his final good-bye, Rex was shocked to see his father lying in the casket wearing the old Yankees baseball jacket with the cap in his hand. He told me, "Dad is revving high rpms in his grave . . . he was a big Mets fan."

Visitation/Viewing: Visitation is a custom that used to take place in the parlors of private homes of the deceased. That is why mortuaries came to be known as "funeral parlors." Back then, burying people was a sideline. The undertaker was often the shoe cobbler, the druggist, the local barber, or some other well-known townsperson.

A viewing of the body is an optional event, which typically takes place a day or two before the service. Friends are invited to view the body and visit with the family. Visitation times and the location are usually listed in the published obituary. Some families and close friends hold a private viewing in the funeral home so they can spend special time with the deceased prior to burial. Since visitation and viewing are personal choices, let your loved ones know your preferences, and talk to them, if possible, about their desires.

Are they comfortable with an open casket? Are there items they would want displayed at the viewing? At some visitations, I've seen photos of the deceased displayed. Are there pictures or items of interest that you would like present at your visitation?

I was five years old when my Grampa died at age ninety-four. He was "laid out" in the parlor of our home, under the picture window. He and I had made bread together every Wednesday morning, so to me it looked like he was resting in a big "bread pan." Friends and neighbors who came by to visit brought flowers from their gardens and home-cooked food. As kids will do, even on the most somber of occasions, my brothers and sister and I got rowdy. To settle us down, Mom gave each of us a lollipop. Mine was root beer, and my sister wanted it. She chased me around the house and into the side yard. I ran back into the parlor and hid my lollipop in Grampa's bread pan, right under his white satin pillow. It was safe there.

The next day, after the procession to the cemetery, when they lowered Grampa into the ground, I burst into tears. "I want my lollipop."

Mom tried to comfort me, not understanding the real reason for my tears. When I explained, she lovingly told me, "Grampa is going to be so happy when he gets to heaven and discovers your root beer lollipop under his pillow."

Then I cried out, "Oh, I wish I had put in a lollipop for Gramma."

Having the Casket in the Funeral Service: Some people have strong feelings about whether it is proper to have a casket present in a funeral service and, if so, whether it should be open or closed. At my father's memorial service, we honored his wishes and held it without his body present. A few of his elderly friends scolded me for not letting them see my father's corpse to say good-bye. Their remarks would have made Dad laugh. He thought the custom of laying out the dead for viewing was gruesome. Many people feel that an open coffin during the funeral service or at the visitation offers a form of closure for the bereaved.

Another trend that helps some people find closure is the personalization of the coffin. Like the plaster casts worn on broken limbs and signed by friends, such coffins take many forms. This same practice is sometimes encouraged at the death of a popular person, where friends or classmates autograph, write poems, or draw pictures on the casket. When a beloved college drama coach died, many of those attending the funeral had been former students. The white casket rested on a metal stand at the front of the church. After the service, the pianist played a special medley as the casket was wheeled out the center aisle of the sanctuary. Everyone stood up and spontaneously applauded.

Pallbearers: Another word for coffin is *pall*. The name pall-bearer, describes those who carry or accompany the coffin during a funeral service. The honor of serving as a pallbearer is usually reserved for special friends or family members. You can decide now whom you want to serve in this capacity and include this list in your Going-Away File, along with their addresses and phone numbers. If you prefer, the mortuary can hire pallbearers or you can opt not to have them.

When five-year-old Chad was about to go to his first funeral, his father felt he should prepare him with a brief description of what the ceremony would be like. He explained that after the service, pallbearers would carry the casket out of the church. During the service, Chad whispered to his mother, "Where are the *bear* outfits?"

Flowers: Some folks believe funeral flowers are a waste of money. My mother felt that way. She used to tell me, "Let me enjoy flowers while I can still see them and smell them. I have no need for them when I am dead." Later I came to realize that flowers create a sense of living beauty and peace for the grieving as well as for others attending the service. At one service I attended, I was told that over three hundred flower arrangements were sent to the church, the family, and the funeral home. There are those who want the simplicity of few flowers, while others want a roomful. Let your family know if you have a preference. In the "Wizard of Id" comic strip in the *Houston Chronicle* in June 1998, the characters were reading the obituary for a local florist: "In lieu of flowers send money."

A record should be kept of all gifts of flowers and who sent them. Each one should be acknowledged. Although writing notes is a big chore, I have heard family members of the deceased say it was therapeutic. Who would you ask now to keep records of flowers and gifts and help write acknowledgment notes after your memorial service?

Years ago, neighbors and friends brought flowers from their own gardens—pansies, peonies, lilacs, or sweet peas—to the home or mortuary. But that practice has long since vanished. At my memorial service, I wish that ritual could return. Instead of the usual commercial funeral arrangements, I think it would be a lovely idea for some of those attending to bring bouquets from their gardens or a potted plant. Or plant a tree in my honor. I'd like that.

Selecting the Location: The location of the funeral or memorial service can affect the emotional impact of the ceremony for those attending. The traditional location for a memorial service is at a church or a funeral home. A church service can be more comfortable for some survivors, who may take solace in being in familiar surroundings. At my father's death, we held a less formal service in the chapel of Carmel Manor Nursing Home where he had lived his last five years. When one of my clients' mother died, only a private graveside service was held, with an informal reception afterward at a country club. Services can also be held in the chapel of the hospital.

After the death of a Vietnam veteran, his widow asked the funeral home to dress him in his marine uniform with all his medals. Visitation and the open casket were held in the church parlor where light refreshments were served before the funeral service in the church sanctuary, with a closed casket present.

Envision your own service; visualize your family, speakers, the music, and your friends as they take it all in—reminiscing about you and your life. Where do you see all of this taking place? What kind of setting would be just right? Plans that include a viewing or a reception will also affect the choice of location for the service. The number of people expected to attend will influence the choice of location, as well as any additional accommodations that may be needed, such as handicap access or kitchen facilities. It's a personal choice. Talk it over with your family so they will have the benefit of your ideas and wishes, and put it all in your Going-Away Plan.

OPTIONS TO CONSIDER: THE SERVICE

Three handsome adult siblings sat in my office looking very grim. "What brings you here today?" I asked.

Troy, the only male, spoke first. "Our mother is in the hospital after suffering a second serious heart attack."

Ginger, a slender blond interrupted. "Doctors told us we should get Mom's affairs in order and make final arrangements. We don't agree on where to hold a funeral service. That's the problem. Mom and I are Baptists, and I think it only appropriate to hold the service in the Baptist church."

Nicole spoke up. "I'm the youngest and nobody listens to me.

Since Troy is the oldest and the executor of Mom's estate, he thinks he can make all the decisions. He's a Buddhist, and he wants to hold the service in his temple. I'm married to a French Catholic from Louisiana, and Mother enjoyed going to church with us. She told me the Catholic rituals are so lovely, and I would like to honor her by having a memorial service in my Catholic church. I think that would please her."

I'm sure I looked a bit surprised at these three sparring adults. "Your mother must be a very special lady. She raised three strong, independent children. And each of you wants to celebrate her life in your own unique way. I admire you. From what I hear, you all want to hold a memorial service and do not plan to have a casket in the church." They all nodded.

"Would you all agree to hold a memorial service in some neutral setting?"

No way, they all said at once.

"Could you support each other in planning three separate services that would reflect your own special beliefs? You may have to coordinate the timing if you plan to attend each other's services." I could see them relax.

Troy smiled, "That's a great idea. We could each arrange to have a memorial service in our own place of worship. I even think Mom would like that. She always supported each of us."

Ginger and Nicole wondered what people would think. I reminded them that it would be unusual, but they were unusual people. Each of them could design a service that would honor their mother in their own distinct way.

They started to laugh at the idea. Their mother died three weeks later, and they followed the plan that began in my office.

This story had a beautiful ending, but most such "real-life" accounts never end. The conflicts are not resolved, the funeral services (whatever they are) are endured, and the pain lingers on—long after the death. One reason preplanning your own service is so important is that it will relieve your loved ones of having to decide what you would have wanted.

One evening while we were visiting with a couple in their home, the subject of this book came up. The husband said he wanted a full-fledged funeral with an open casket and his photo displayed, a long procession to the cemetery, and a big reception afterward. His wife looked at him in surprise. "I didn't know that." His response was interesting. "I never realized the importance of sharing my ideas about this until we discussed Margie's book."

Would it surprise you to learn that many people are now planning their own funeral services? What disturbs me is the number of folks who have specific ideas about this subject but have not revealed them to even their closest family members. Many think that it would be audacious. Others view the concept as a real opportunity and realize that taking charge of your own final exit is a rewarding responsibility.

The idea of planning your own memorial service may seem unusual, but how many funerals have you left thinking, "That was not at all like Sally (or Paul . . .). If she had planned her funeral, it would have been totally different"? Of course. And wouldn't it have been better if it *had* been more like Sally? And if it's true of Sally, then the more your service is like *you,* the likelier it is that those attending will be genuinely comforted. What kind of finale would you prefer? It could be a traditional formal service with the emphasis on scriptures that provide comfort. A full religious service might reflect your faith and the devotion of your family. If that seems too formal, you might want a celebration of your life in a typical memorial service, or one that was totally unusual, say like a pre-recorded video of yourself addressing those who attend your service. You're doing the planning, so it's all up to you. And you should present it exactly the way you want it to happen.

Perhaps you already know what ingredients and atmosphere you would like in your service. If so, write a full description and discuss it with your loved ones. A funeral is a statement that a death has occurred. But more importantly, it is a celebration that a life has been lived. If your thoughts are still formulating, check through the following items for features you may want to include.

Music: What types of musical *performers* do you prefer—choir, congregational, special (solo, duet, etc.), or instrumental? What types of music would be most like you—traditional religious, contemporary religious, classical, or country? You may want to choose the specific musicians and songs for your service based on the above preferences.

Solo music can enhance the ceremony as can congregational singing. Our daughter Toby would like someone to sing the black spiritual "Swing Low, Sweet Chariot." One of my favorites is "His Eye Is on the Sparrow." And my closest friends will know I planned the service when songs from *The Sound of Music* fill the sanctuary. Trumpets, harps, and bagpipes have highlighted some services. At my father's memorial service, the Carmelite Sisters played their guitars and sang "I Know Nothing of Tomorrow, Except the Love of God Will Rise Before the Sun." What are your choices?

Special Readings: Poetry or other literary selections can be both stirring and comforting. Special readings will reflect your personal tastes as well as your concern for your loved ones and friends you are leaving behind. Scripture is read at most funerals; select passages that mean the most to you. Remember that Scripture read at the funeral will draw people's minds to you, your faith, and the inspiration you provided while you were alive. Clergy can help with suggestions, if you need their input.

Dad wanted me to read Ecclesiastes 3:1–8, and recite the poem "My Get Up and Go Has Got Up and Went."

My Get Up and Go Has Got Up and Went

How do I know that my youth is all spent?
Well, my get up and go has got up and went.
But in spite of it all, I am able to grin
When I recall where all my get up has been.

Old age is golden, so I've heard it said
But sometimes I wonder when I get into bed
With my ears in a drawer, and my teeth in a cup,
My eyes on a table until I wake up.
'Ere sleep dims my eyes, I say to myself,

"Is there anything *else* I should lay on the shelf?"
But I'm happy to say as I close my door,
My friends are the same, perhaps even more.

When I was young, my slippers were red
And I could kick my heels right over my head.
When I grew older, my slippers were blue
But I could dance the whole night through.

Now I am old, my slippers are black
I walk to the store and puff my way back.
But the reason I know that my youth is all spent
My get up and go has got up and went.

But I really don't mind, when I think with a grin
Of all the grand places my get up has been.

Since I have retired from life's competition
I busy myself with complete repetition.

I get up each morning and dust off my wits,
Pick up the paper and read the "obits."
If my name is missing, I know I'm not dead
So I eat a good breakfast and go back to bed.

—Anonymous

Eulogy: This is one part of the service you may not want to write yourself. Someone else would be free to say things that might sound self-serving coming from your own pen. Eulogies usually provide a personal touch—giving praise and acclaim and describing positive characteristics. Family and friends also appreciate interesting and humorous tributes to the deceased.

You might suggest people to give testimonials at your memorial service. You could ask them now if they would be willing to participate. Most people are honored to be asked. At Erma Bombeck's service, her children told heartwarming, amusing stories about their mother, the well-known columnist. Sam, who planned his funeral several years before his death at ninety-two, asked a group of special people to speak on different aspects of his life. They were thrilled and carried out his wishes with love: His best friend spoke on what Sam was like as a friend; his grandson spoke on Sam the grandfather; one of his Sunday school students on Sam the teacher, etc. It created a service filled with amazing memories, humorous stories, and inspiring hope. What interesting stories could be told about you? Who could tell them best?

Besides the clergy and chosen family and friends, would you like to open up your memorial service to spontaneous comments from anyone in the audience who would like to share memories of you? This informality can add a great deal of charm and intimacy to a service.

At Dad's service, I shared his philosophy of life and what I had learned from him. One of his humorous lessons was, "Two things you need to enjoy life to the fullest: (1) moderation in all things, and (2) don't waste energy resisting temptations." My husband, Jenks, shared a story about Dad and a special "ring ceremony." My father had presented him a ruby ring that he had worn since receiving it as a college graduation gift in 1910. Jenks recalled how they sat together on a bench in the garden of Carmel Manor. Dad told Jenks he was like a son to him and that he wanted him to have the ring. It was a very touching story and tears came to his eyes as Jenks recalled that emotional event.

Sermon/Affirmation: You should have exceptional confidence in whomever you select to provide spiritual affirmation. Although you may not tell him or her everything to say, there may be specific thoughts, situations, beliefs, incidents, etc., that you would like included or excluded. You should make them known, and you should feel free to suggest both theme and favorite scriptures for this part of the service. For instance, a colleague told me she wanted her memorial service to be a reflection of her belief that death was a release from the pain of her five-year battle with cancer. After the service, everyone gathered in the church courtyard, the minister read Psalm 23, then everyone released multicolored balloons high above the church steeple.

Audiovisual Presentation: Slides presenting the life of the deceased or video presentations can be uplifting and emotional. Go ahead now and pull together photos and slides that would present the story of your life in the way you would want to be remembered. It can be a fun family project. Sitting around the kitchen table looking at photos and remembering experiences can be a wonderful gift to everyone involved. That kind of sharing creates a living legacy and carries on the family heritage.

You may even record a video message of yourself, talking to your family, friends, and the whole audience. It may be emotionally difficult for some people to see the deceased person alive on the screen, but in what better way could you convey your love, affection, and reassurances. Such a video could become a cherished possession.

Good narration and appropriate music can also greatly enhance a slide or audio presentation. Who might you choose who will add that special joy to your presentation? You may want to recruit some professional help for this project. Can you visualize your family and loved ones sitting together viewing this special video and treasuring every moment?

Specific Requests: Funerals are becoming more personalized and unique. They range anywhere from a simple service to a catered event, including an honor guard or a twenty-one-gun salute. There are those who request that communion be served.

Occasionally unusual requests are made. Four-legged creatures played a part in the New York memorial service for Linda McCartney, an avid animal-rights activist. Her love of horses was shown when two of her Shetland ponies were led to the front of the church. A young girl then rode her brown-and-white Appaloosa down the carpeted aisle of Riverside Church. At one funeral for a man who died at age fifty, the family passed out a list of fifty meaningful events in his life. When five-year-old Kimberly died of leukemia, her kindergarten classmates sang at the service. Afterward, everyone released pink balloons.

Printed Program: A printed program provides the order of service, and it can also contain information about the deceased and sometimes the published obituary. I have seen a ten-page program that included the life, accomplishments, and pictures of the deceased with a personal history. Others are one-page bulletins. If you want to use a program, start a file of programs from services you liked, which can serve as a simple guide later.

Other Ideas: A guest-signing book is usually in the foyer at the location of the service. It can be comforting for the family to review the names of those who attended. Someone would need to be on hand to invite the people to sign the book. A special person to welcome the guests adds a lovely tone to the service. Mortuary or church personnel could also handle this duty.

As you plan your personal service, you may want to include items that are not listed here. Your memorial should be whatever you would like for a celebration of your life and could include things such as flags, fraternal or military regalia, etc.

When I tell my family about all the songs, poems, and stories I want at my service, they remind me that a five-hour service is a bit long. But I have fun thinking about all the details I want at my Going-Away Party. And I think you will, too.

OPTIONS TO CONSIDER:
FUNERAL PROCESSION TO GRAVE SITE

Funeral processions can take many forms. Sometimes people simply walk to a nearby cemetery. Cars often follow the hearse to the grave site. Some folks have requested a brass band to accompany the procession. In larger cities, the law requires a paid police escort for a long cortege.

There is a story about four women who were returning from a shopping trip and accidentally got trapped in a lengthy funeral procession. They were afraid to turn off for fear all the cars behind them would follow them. They ended up attending a graveside service for a complete stranger.

Some cultures and faiths have processions that are just short of a theatrical production, which can provide a release for many emotions. The funeral procession for the "king of the gypsies" is one I will always remember from my childhood. Music blared and people clapped. The body was visible in a majestic glass carriage, pulled by four sleek chestnut horses on their way to Evergreen Cemetery. From the front porch of our home in Southgate, Kentucky, we watched the long caravan of fancy, flower-decorated cars, with license plates from all over the country, meander along to the grave site. My reaction: "Now that's going out in style."

A small tribe in Bali has a special funeral tradition of carrying the casket through town, while everyone follows. To relieve tension and sadness, pallbearers drop the casket as often as possible, and all the people laugh. When they drop it in water, there is even more hilarity.

Would a procession to the graveside be appropriate after your memorial service? Seeing the black hearse waiting at the side door of a church after a funeral is an impressive sight. Instead of somber black funeral cars, however, I always wished they would use a white hearse or, better yet, multicolored ones. Can you imagine a funeral procession driving along the freeway on its way to the cemetery . . . and the hearse and family car are bright red or pink or purple? Most places might not be ready for that, but white might be nice.

OPTIONS TO CONSIDER: GRAVESIDE SERVICE

A graveside ceremony can also bring a final few minutes of comfort to your loved ones. One person asked a friend to dress up as a clown to entertain those attending the service and hand out colorful balloons. Another requested guitar music and group singing. At one ceremony, the family threw vegetable seeds into the grave to honor their father who for many years had enjoyed planting and harvesting a vegetable garden.

Graveside services are optional and, if held, are typically brief. They can be private or public. Usually one includes Scripture reading, prayer, and maybe throwing rose petals on the casket as it is lowered into the ground. This service may be the final meeting for some family and friends, especially if the grave is a long distance from their homes.

OPTIONS TO CONSIDER: RECEPTION

A reception after a memorial or funeral service provides a place where people can remember, talk, and feel connected to others who cared about the deceased. It allows those gathered to recall joyful events from their loved one's life and re-creates loving memories. It can be held in a church parlor, private home, garden, museum, or restaurant, and it can reflect some aspect of the deceased's personality, just as the service did.

At the "going-away party" for Charles Schulz, creator of the "Peanuts" comic strip, the crowd was offered chocolate chip cookies and root beer—standard fare for Snoopy and the "Peanuts gang" after their games.

Do you want a reception held in your honor? What place would be special for your family and friends to celebrate your life? What food or refreshments would you like served? One friend requested that champagne and apricot Brie be offered. This can also be a time for showing special videos or a slide presentation of the deceased, which adds a warm intimate experience. Be creative. You can plan a memorial service and reception that will be a going-away party remembered long after you are gone. Who would you want to be in charge of that celebration?

Some people prefer a simple reception or open house to celebrate the life of the deceased with no formal service. At this occasion, usually tributes are made and toasts are offered, and those attending share stories and memories of their loved one. There are many options. Write down your ideas, and include them as a part of your Going-Away File.

OPTIONS TO CONSIDER: CEO

You may not always be in charge of your life, but you can make plans to be in charge of your death. After completing all the plans for your memorial service, you will want to be confident that someone will make sure your wishes are carried out after you die. One way to put your mind at ease about this is to talk to an especially trusted family member or friend. Go over your plans, both orally and with a written copy, and ask the person to take responsibility for assuring that they will be followed. The person you designate will be your CEO—your Chief *Exit* Officer.

Who would be that person for you? You can ask someone now so that he or she can enjoy the title . . . and share your plans. Also, make sure your whole family knows about your plans and your CEO. This will keep surprises to a minimum and contribute to a more relaxed atmosphere before and during your service.

A study coauthored by Dr. Elizabeth Lamont and Dr. Nicholas Christakis showed that doctors are not only bad at making predictions about how long a patient will live, but also are uncomfortable passing on information to patients when the message is discouraging. Dr. Christakis noted, "Part of the reason we die badly is because we don't see death coming, so we don't plan accordingly."[1]

You can't know how long you will live, but preparing for your final exit gives you the chance to take charge and make important decisions so your survivors will know your wishes when that time comes.

When Dad was ninety years old, a newspaper reporter asked him if he had lived all of his life in Kentucky. He replied, "Not yet."

11

The Good-Bying Process

It was time for Pop Little and me to make one of the hardest decisions in life.

I knew any long-distance call from Kentucky could be bad news. After all, my father was ninety-five. In the twelve years since Mother had died, he had been living alone in the house where I grew up. Only a month before this call, in May 1979, Jenks and I and our four children, their spouses, and two grandkids had arrived in Kentucky from all over the country. We had celebrated Dad's ninety-fifth birthday in his "old Kentucky home." The celebration brought out his sense of humor and his enthusiasm for life.

Being stone deaf for the last twenty-five years had not slowed him down, but old age had. Writing notes was the only way to communicate with him, so pens and paper were scattered all over the house. Dad kept a notepad and pencil in his pocket at all times. He had been a favorite history teacher and high-school principal back in 1916, so many friends and neighbors took good care of him and visited him often.

Now, a month later, his special neighbors, Hilda and Ervin Greis, two of Dad's angels, called me to say Dad was not doing well. "We stopped by his house this evening, and he was sitting in the dark, unshaven, with a big gash over one eye. He had fallen and hit his head on the corner of the kitchen table, knocking him out. He didn't want us to bother you, but we think you should come home. He is depressed and has lost his spirit, which is unlike him. We don't think he should be living alone anymore."

In past years we had invited my father to live with us in Houston, but he always declined. He didn't want to live with us or with my sister, Fran, in California. Had he changed his mind? I would discover more when I got to Southgate. This trip would be different from my regular visits. The agenda would not be a celebration, but a time of decision.

Conversations with Dad through the years had often included discussions about his "going-away party." He once told me if he didn't die soon, there wouldn't be anybody left who knew him. "If you're going to live a long time," he told me, "you better make friends with old age."

When I opened the back door of my childhood home, the familiar smell of Prince Albert tobacco greeted me. A good sign. But I found Dad slumped down in his favorite worn green chair smoking his pipe. He looked worse than I had ever seen him—lonely, and like he had given up on life. He held his pipe in his mouth with shaky fingers and his eyes were closed. Because of his hearing loss, he was unaware his younger daughter was standing by his side.

I touched his arm gently and bent down to kiss him. He hugged me tightly. "I'm glad you're here." His speech was weak. So different from the usual strong, authoritative voice.

I grabbed the old round leather footstool and sat close, with pen and paper ready for conversation. His eyes were now dimmed with cataracts. Printing large letters with a heavy black pen was a necessity.

Dad put a quivering hand on my arm. "I am old. I can't see and can't hear. Parkinson's disease is getting worse. Can't take care of myself anymore. I'm no good to myself or to anybody else. I'm ready to meet my Maker."

"Since your Maker isn't ready for you yet, we'll have to make other plans."

Looking at me through misty blue eyes, Pop shook his head. "Margie, you always come home with ideas in your head. You are going to try to talk me out of dying, aren't you?"

"We're going to talk about a lot of things. But first we'll eat your favorite meal: pancakes, sausage, and strawberry shortcake. I'll come get you when it's ready. Enjoy your pipe."

Familiar family pictures hanging on the walls smiled at me as I walked through the house to the kitchen. As a psychotherapist in Houston, I routinely help clients move through changes in their lives. But thinking about what needed to change for the patriarch of the C. Roy Little family was overwhelming. Tears filled my eyes as pancake batter sizzled on a hot griddle.

We ate at the kitchen table while I wrote on my handy pad. "Tell me about the gash on your head. Looks like you got in a fight and lost." Dad's familiar laugh filled the room.

"All I know is little Tony, the four-year-old neighbor boy, came in to wish me happy Father's Day and found me on the floor. His parents told me he ran home crying, 'Mr. Little is lying on the floor and won't talk to me.' They rushed me to the hospital, but there was nothing seriously wrong. I must of tripped on something and fallen. I had a bang-up Father's Day. Stirred up the neighbors."

He paused. "I can't live alone anymore. But I want to stay in Kentucky. Find a place around here where I will be cared for and no one will have to worry about me. Now let's sit on the back porch glider so I can smoke a cigar. Your sister, Fran, thinks my smoking is going to shorten my life." He laughed, unhooked his cane from behind the chair, and slowly made his way out the back door.

Together we watched squirrels and chipmunks scamper around the yard. His wrinkled hand touched my arm. "I don't want to leave my old Kentucky home, but I've lived here as long as I can. I'm very dependent now. Can't do much for myself anymore. It's not a good feeling. I'm not scared of dying; I'm just tired of living."

In big letters I wrote, "I get tired of living, too, sometimes. We'll talk more about all of these things tomorrow." Hand in hand we sat in silence while the creak of the swaying glider kept me company. A chorus of locusts made music that Dad could no longer hear. Fireflies flickered as darkness began to settle in. I used to catch them when I was a kid, but I don't see them in Houston. Too hot, I guess. Dad was focused on the same memory. "Remember the lightning bugs you kept in a mayonnaise jar over there on that porch table?"

PLANNING THE MOVE

After checking out several nursing homes, I took Dad to visit Carmel Manor. It sits high above the bend in the river in Fort Thomas, Kentucky, ten minutes from his home. The gray stone building is surrounded by acres of woods and wildlife. Its round towers at the corners resemble a feudal castle. Blooming tulips and irises welcomed us along their winding roadway approach. We went into the office, talked to Mother Superior, and took care of the preliminaries.

Later we sat on a bench and gazed across the Ohio River at Cincinnati's familiar landmarks. Dad announced, "It won't be easy for me to live here or any place, but it's time. Carmel Manor looks pretty fancy, but it's a good choice. When can I move in?"

I told him there was a two-week wait for a room, but we had a lot to do during that time. He nodded his head. We drove back to his home to get ready for the move.

The following morning, we sat in the kitchen of his home and talked about the furnishings in the room. I turned on a recorder to tape our conversation. "What's that thing?" Dad asked.

I explained on my yellow pad. He shook his head in amazement. "What a miraculous gadget. So what we say will be recorded for posterity? I better watch my language."

THE GOOD-BYING PROCESS

I used the recorder to tape Dad's voice explaining things to me. Recording conversations like this serves several purposes. It is usually difficult to remember all the words spoken when you ask important questions. The recording reminds you of what was said and helps recall special comments that were exchanged. It also can be comforting to just hear the voice of a beloved person after their death. Some folks may be afraid of having their conversation recorded and would tell you to turn it off. Others might tell you to turn up the volume. Since Dad had been a teacher most of his life and was comfortable talking in front of people, the recorder did not scare him.

While we sat in the kitchen, I said, "Tell me about this table and the pie safe in the corner. Where did they come from?"

He cleared his throat and sat up straight. His voice was stronger now, and his eyes came alive. "This is kind of like being on radio. I've never been on the air before. You think of everything. Now about this table. My mother, your grandmother, Kate Fish Little, gave it to us when your mom and I married in 1913. As a boy, I ate a lot of buckwheat cakes at this table in Oregon, Illinois. My mother took in boarders when I was young, so we always had a crowd eating together. I still remember some of their names: Olaf Carlson, Shadrack Bond, and Erhard Burger. My older sister, Ora, sat on this side between Carlson and me. Many folks from the old country seemed to end up rooming at our house.

"Since we acquired this table, your mother and I have moved it around the country. You made pull-taffy here and your brothers bottled their homemade root beer on it. They laid the bottles under the stove to 'ripen.' That was good stuff. Your mother put on new oilcloth every spring and she rolled out her piecrusts here. Our family ate a lot of your mother's good old cooking around this table." I could almost taste Mom's tarty blackberry pies made from the buckets of berries Dad and I picked in the woods behind our house.

"That pie safe came from your mother's family, just like these chairs. And she learned to cane the chair seats when they wore out. She was a talented woman." Tears filled his eyes. "It's been twelve years since she died. It's lonely without her. But I've done pretty well, with the help of neighbors."

He pointed to the cabinet. "Don't know much about that cupboard. The bright-colored Fiesta ware was always stacked in there. There are a lot of nice things in this house that came from your mother's side of the family." He paused. "I'll miss this kitchen."

Humming, the cassette recorded a long silence. Dad nodded toward the window. "I sit here and watch the birds. Sometimes there are ten different varieties at the feeder. They've come to depend on me to feed them year round. My grandfather, Isaac Fish, taught me to stick a cob of corn in the birdbath in the winter. When the water freezes, birds can suck water through the cob. Usually there's a family of rabbits somewhere in the yard. Haven't seen them lately. I like to watch God's creatures." A faraway look came over his eyes. "My animal friends will miss me. Time now for a nap."

A lot of good-bying awaited us, but we had started the process. In the days ahead, Dad and I would sit in other rooms and talk about their contents. Since Dad's yard was special to him, I knew we would walk around outside. And go to the basement and the garage, as well as the attic closet. Good thing we had two weeks before his room was ready at the nursing home. That was barely long enough.

I was glad I had brought several cassette tapes with me from Texas. Dad seemed to enjoy talking about his belongings and having our conversations recorded. "I wish I could listen to the tape," he told me. "I miss out on a lot of things not being able to hear. Can't hear the birds. But I don't hear babies cry, so that's good. In my ninety-five years, I've heard a lot. Did you hear about that old-timer who got new hearing aids? He told a friend he was hearing things he never expected to hear. The friend said, 'Your family must be pleased.' The old man replied, 'I haven't told them yet.'"

After naptime we sat in the "front room" at his roll-top desk. "Where did you get this huge thing? It has always dominated the room."

He patted the desk lovingly. "I bought it for five dollars from Procter and Gamble in Cincinnati in 1921, when they modernized. It's been my office ever since. It has nineteen drawers. Can you find the secret compartments?"

I explored the cubbyholes, each one filled with special memories. A Greek medal he had won in college. His glee club pin. A picture of him with students he taught in Beirut, Syria, in 1910. Names written on the back sounded like the United Nations. The cigar box that served as the family "bank" was still in the top right-hand drawer. Among coins scattered on the bottom of the box was a scrap of paper. In a child's handwriting, a scribbled note read "IOU 6 cents, Margie." As kids, when we borrowed money from the cigar box, we left our IOUs. When I showed the note to Dad, he laughed. "Guess you still owe the bank."

An old manual adding machine sat on top of the desk. When I played store as a kid, I pulled down the handle to add up the cost of things. A can of Prince Albert tobacco rested next to a rack full of pipes. In the bottom drawer was a brown envelope of pictures from his journeys in the Holy Land. One showed him with a mustache, walking along the desert clutching a small Persian rug he had purchased at the market. I was surprised how good looking Dad was with a mustache. The threadbare Oriental runner was still in the upstairs hallway.

In a small secret compartment in the lower left-hand corner of the old desk, I discovered a gold locket containing an attractive young girl's picture. "Who is this?" I asked.

"Oh, that's Edna Houston. We went to first grade together. She kept in touch through the years." Dad held the trinket in his hand. "I'd forgotten all about her. Your mother didn't like me keeping that picture. Edna got old and died some years ago." He leaned his gray head against the back of the chair. "You know, I don't remember getting old."

Dad shuffled slowly to the living room where the piano used to be. "Good thing you took the piano back to Kansas with you years ago. With my arthritic fingers I couldn't play anymore and I can't hear. I miss music. You four kids used to sit here with me while I played. Bingo (our dog) sat alongside of us. He knew good music when he heard it, and would howl. We'd sing, 'My Bonnie Lies Over the Ocean' and 'My Old Kentucky Home.' I always played by ear, but you all thought I was a real maestro.

"Did you know I helped build that piano? I worked in the piano factory after I quit high school at age fourteen. That was a dumb thing to do. To drop out of school. But I thought I knew it all then." Dad shook his head in disgust at himself. "I paid twenty-three dollars for the piano in 1913. Your mother was a fine musician. Played the organ in the college church where I was the janitor. I'd watch her practice while I cleaned the sanctuary. I fell in love with her and the music she could make. Now let's sit on the couch and look through these books I stacked on the table."

Many of the books were leather-bound volumes from another century. He sorted through the stack until he pulled out one. "Here's a book of blue limericks that your Houston friend Nancy sent me. Your mother disapproved of the verses, but I enjoyed them." I was glad to know his sense of humor was still intact.

Another day we chatted while sitting at the round dining table. I brought in two glasses of lemonade and some cookies. With all the doors and windows open, even the transom, a warm breeze blew through the room and reminded me that summers can be hot in Kentucky.

"What will you miss most in this room?" I asked.

Tears came. "Leaving this home is like tearing my heart out. I don't know if I can do it. I have lived here nearly sixty-five years. This house is full of memories. I wanted to die here like your mother did."

For a few seconds, the only sounds recorded were the sobs we shared. Then Dad blew his nose, wiped his eyes with a torn handkerchief, and took a sip of lemonade. He straightened himself in his chair and pointed to my favorite piece in the corner.

"That cherry desk belonged to your mother's Great-Grandfather Weaver who lived in Weaversville, Pennsylvania." As he explained its history, memories raced through my head. Dad put his hand on my arm again. "When you were a kid, you wanted to get rid of that desk and all of your mother's antiques, and buy some fancy things from Sears. You didn't know much back then."

He pointed to another corner of the dining room. Your mother kept that Singer sewing machine humming, making most of the clothes for you and Fran. After your brother graduated from West Point, he left his heavy academy overcoat here. Your mom cut it up and made you a suit with gold buttons down the front. When you wore it to school, you were quite a hit. All your prom dresses came off that sewing machine. She even made a prom dress for one of your friends. Now let's walk outside. I'll get my cane." I put the strap of the recorder around my neck and we headed out.

The screen door banged shut behind us as we made our way out to the low stone wall. Dad whacked the stones with his cane. "Before you were born, your brothers and I built this wall. Purple phlox bloomed along the edge when your mother was alive. She was in charge of flowers. I was in charge of the vegetable garden. This whole backyard was my garden for many years. Little by little it has gotten smaller. Now I can't do any of it. Makes me sad to feel so useless."

Sitting on the stone wall, Dad counted the trees that surrounded us. "Forty-three trees in all. And I planted most of them myself, some of them from seeds. When you were born I planted that redbud tree. You both have grown well. The big walnut tree was planted when your brother John was a youngster. When he was lost during the war in 1943, I nailed a marker on it to commemorate his life. When Amanda (my first grandchild) was born in 1976, I planted that mimosa tree. You and Jenks planted all those dogwood trees in the side yard. They were good birthday presents. I'll miss this yard."

To steady us both, I put my arm around his waist as we wandered across the side yard. He stopped near the birdbath. Using his cane, he carefully poked around some loose grass and then got down on his hands and knees. With a small stick, he lifted up a furry ball and said, "Looky here. Baby bunnies. Five of them I think." I knelt down beside him and saw tiny ears sticking out of a hole. "I've been looking for them," Dad said. "Usually the bunnies eat my lettuce leaves when they first come out of the ground. There won't be any garden to feed them this year."

Our "good-bying" took us toward the basement as Dad talked on about his memories. We cautiously navigated the rickety stairs, sat on the bottom step, and looked around at the bare walls. "Remember when someone gave you a puppy? You were afraid we wouldn't let you keep it, so you hid it in the washing machine. Not a good place for a puppy. Over on those shelves, your mother lined up her canned stuff: blackberry jam, spiced peaches, and tomato relish. During the winter, we kept a bushelbasket full of apples down here. Every summer I made you kids whitewash the cellar walls. Kept you out of trouble, and it looked really nice when you finished."

Near the end of the waiting period, we sat on a wooden trunk in the long, narrow attic closet. A bare light bulb shone above us. I pulled out a big box and discovered it was full of pictures. I told Dad we would go through them in the evenings after supper. I knew he was the only one who could identify most of the old photographs, some dating back to his childhood. An odd-shaped, tattered carton with tan tissue paper hanging out caught my eye and jolted my memory. I knew the Egyptian mummy hand had lived in that box all of my childhood days. I remembered holding that unique object, touching the long skinny fingers and imagining it belonged to an Egyptian princess. But I knew it was no longer there.

LETTING GO

By the end of the two weeks, baby bunnies skidoodled around the yard, with mother rabbit close by. We knew the time was near for Dad to leave this place. We sat close on the porch swing. "I wish

Jenks was here," he mumbled softly. Then he took my hand. "It's hard to let go, but these last two weeks have been some of the happiest times of my life. We've shared so many memories. Things I'd forgotten. It was good to look at everything and talk about old times. You have helped me say good-bye to my old Kentucky home. Now I'm ready to go."

When I called Jenks in Houston, he was involved in important meetings but said he would come to Kentucky as soon as he could get away.

Carmel Manor called to say Dad's room was ready. We packed a small suitcase and made our plans to leave the next day. After living in the same home for sixty-five years, it's impossible just to put your life in a bag and leave. You walk out the door and close it behind you, but something of you will always be there.

As we drove down the driveway, Dad looked back: "Good-bye, house. Good-bye, trees and yard. Good-bye, bunnies. Hope you'll have a good life here. This has been a wonderful place to raise my family."

Tears streamed down his cheeks, and I was relieved he couldn't hear my sobbing. We drove away to Dad's new home after that one last look at 256 Linden Avenue in Southgate, Kentucky.

SIMPLIFYING THE GOOD-BYING PROCESS

The situation at the time of *your* approaching death will not be exactly like Dad's, but his story includes many experiences and emotions that are common to all in the good-bying process.

Whatever the characteristics of your own path may be, there are some things you can do now to prepare for the transition—preparations that will make it easier and more meaningful for you and the loved ones who tread that path with you.

Resist the Resistance to Change: People tend to resist change, especially when they get older. Dad often told me how comfortable he felt in the house he had lived in for so long. "I can feel my way around even when I can't see well. Everything about a new place will be unfamiliar, and I don't like the idea of getting used to strange surroundings."

Sometimes resistance to change keeps you in a place too long, making it increasingly difficult to adjust to a new environment. It can blur your vision to possibilities for making life easier. Too often it takes an emergency, like a fall or a disabling illness, to make it clear that changing living arrangements is the very best thing. However, if you are willing to make changes before a catastrophe, usually you will have more options, and you can be involved in the choices.

Accept Reality: Accepting reality is essential to a healthy good-bying process. Age changes things. That's a reality. You will have less and less control of the world around you as you approach the end of the line. That's a reality. But many of my counselees seem to be afraid that they will hasten the event by accepting the inevitable. The opposite is more likely. When you look "good-bying" straight in the eye and acknowledge it as a normal stage of life, its power to intimidate is reduced, and so are your anxieties. Then, as your anxieties lessen, you will have more energy to live a fuller life—and probably a longer one. It's not too early right *now* to accept the reality that the good-bying process *will* take place.

Acknowledge That Dependency Will Happen: The time will come when you will have to entrust the decisions about your life to someone else. I definitely am not suggesting that you throw in the towel too early. It is both vital and beneficial for you to hold on to your independence as long as you can be *safely self-supporting.* But one of the best things you can do to prepare for those days or years when you will be dependent is to acknowledge *now* that *dependency* *will happen.* If you stay in denial until some tragedy renders you helpless, adjusting to dependency is likely to be traumatic. If you have mentally and emotionally processed the likelihood of such a phase, you will transition and adapt better when dependency becomes the best way for you to live.

Independent people have a difficult time letting go or allowing others to help. A common myth is that depending on others is a sign of insignificance. It is important to remember that you have been contributing to other's lives for many years: caring for them, giving of yourself in many ways to make the world a better place. Depending on others—like when you accept help from your church, Meals on Wheels, Medicare, or Medicaid—does not make you worthless or inconsequential. The purpose of these programs is to make life easier for folks who need assistance in the later years of life. In most cases, these same people have earned the right to be on the receiving end by living long lives of compassion and helpfulness toward other people.

Being dependent can also cause a sense of helplessness. When Dad could no longer drive, he lost control of a part of his life and the world had new barriers. Most people struggle their entire lives to become independent; accepting help graciously is difficult. So what happens for many elderly is that they refuse to even talk about the possibility of relying on others until, for whatever reason, circumstances force the issue.

A dependence on God and the wonderful gifts that He has bestowed is often taken for granted. Yet, if you stop to think of all the blessings you have received, the thoughts of trusting God to be with you till the end of life—and after death—is a great comfort. God's gifts come in many forms, and people who help other people with their time, energy, and talents are right up there on top of the list of things for which you can be grateful.

My friend Karl, age eighty-one, lived on the farm and prided himself on being totally independent. He had lived through hard times but always made do with whatever he had. Even though Karl was slowing down and getting forgetful, he would not even discuss changing his lifestyle. He knew he didn't see well and had several close calls with his truck, but stubbornness kept him in a place that was unsafe and unhealthy. Arthritis in his hands and legs made it difficult for him to maneuver machinery, and his son tried to get him to move in with him, but Karl wouldn't stop until . . . his tractor hit a tree and mangled his legs. A neighbor found him in the field unable to move. After several complicated operations on both legs, the doctors told his son that Karl would never walk again.

Karl lived out his last years in a nursing care facility where he was dependent on others for every need. He became a disgruntled old man. His son told me, "It didn't have to end like this. I'm so angry at Dad for being so stubborn that I have a hard time even visiting him. It could have been so much easier on him and everybody else if he had paid attention to his failing health and accepted the reality that he was losing control of his ability to handle the farm."

Dependence on others will be challenging, no matter what. Other people won't do things the way you have always done them. A friend told me when her daughter's help becomes awkward, they jokingly kid each other by saying, "The helping hand strikes again." It will be much easier if you can find the humor and kid about it. So talk with your family now and acknowledge candidly to them that you know at some point your life will be in their hands. This openness among family members will ease the transition when you finally have to cross that line.

Maybe that's why someone said, "Be good to your children because they'll be selecting your nursing home."

Understand the Burden on Caregivers: Understanding the

stress on loved ones—the caregivers—helps everyone. It is an added burden for those who care for you when you fail to comprehend what they are going through while they are trying to make your life comfortable. One wife I know permanently damaged her back during years of lifting her husband when he could not take care of himself. Focusing on your own discomfort and being unconscious of how others are adjusting their lives to accommodate you is an easy trap; don't fall into it.

Although Dad was a special kind of man, he was also a chauvinist and often judgmental. Before he moved from his home, my husband and I frequently went to Kentucky to make sure he was all right and to keep his home in good repair. One summer while Jenks was trimming his hedge, fixing the screen door, and cutting the grass, I was cleaning the house, washing, ironing, mending his clothes, cooking, and freezing single servings of food so it would be convenient for him to eat when we were gone.

After working several days at my chores, Dad sat at the table and watched me while I cleaned the kitchen. "Women do a lot of useless work. None of these things you're doing are necessary. But Jenks is outside doing a lot of important things that need doing."

I came close to erupting. But having to take time to write my message to him calmed me a bit. I sat down, grabbed a pen and paper, and scribbled in big bold letters, "I don't like what you said to me. I'm glad you appreciate what Jenks does, but you have no appreciation for all the things that I'm doing to make your life easier. That makes me sad."

He put a shaky hand on my shoulder and shook his head. "You're right, Margie. You do many things for me. I'm sorry I was so thoughtless. I'll try to do better." He looked up with tears in his eyes. "You know, your mother worked hard, but I never appreciated all the things she did. I wish I had been more thoughtful of her."

Everyone needs to be told they are appreciated. If I had not told Dad how I felt, I would have kept a lot of resentment within me and that would not have been good for either of us.

I remember how relieved I felt when Dad suggested he was ready to leave his home and live in a place that would care for him on a daily basis. After his move, our visits were much more relaxed and enjoyable. I could focus on him and not worry about repairing the house, fixing meals, or taking him to doctors.

Of course, it was wonderful that Dad was able to live independently as long as he did after Mom died, but unfortunately, some people stay too long in their home.

Look at Options: The most common and natural arrangement for caregiving is by family members—a spouse or children. Sometimes it's a sibling, another relative, or a good friend who will provide the necessary care for an elderly person. In Dad's case, it was the local Catholic church that came to his rescue. They referred a retired couple to us who wanted to help someone in need. Erv and Hilda Greis were Dad's angels. They refused any payment for their loving care of my father for seven years before he moved into Carmel Manor Nursing Home. Dad's will made them an equal, along with his family, as beneficiaries of his modest estate. There is no doubt in my mind that Dad continued to live independently for all those extra years because of this loving couple.

But what happens when there are no relatives or friends who can help and finances are limited? That's when local social-services agencies or churches may offer assistance, which might include transportation, Meals on Wheels, and home-care help. Check out these possibilities in your area before you have a crisis. I know many churches have a group of folks who find it rewarding to provide assistance to those in need of help.

Usually churches are a good resource for helping people in need. Many of them keep a list of people who are available to assist others with transportation, food, or visitation. They usually know the phone numbers of local agencies that offer assistance. Some churches have a pastoral committee that is organized just for this purpose. The "Stephen Ministry," for instance, is a group of lay people who go through training to learn how to be a blessing to folks in the congregation. If your church does not have the help you need, it is important to know you can call any church in your community.

Because the leaving process usually includes some personal difficulties, it is beneficial to explore all the possibilities. You might discover that talking with a therapist is helpful in sorting out your feelings and making decisions. Alternatives may include having a roommate, living with a friend or relative, or inviting a neighbor to check up on you on a daily basis. If you have financial means, there are other choices.

Wesley and Christine were still relatively healthy when they faced the reality that they needed to simplify living arrangements and have less responsibility. They chose an "independent living facility," where they had a smaller place to care for and planned social activities were scheduled each month. Someone checked on them each day. A year later Wesley developed heart problems, and they needed more assistance. So they moved into the "assisted living" section of the same facility. This area had wheelchair access to bathrooms and a bell to ring for immediate assistance, and two meals a day were offered in the dining room. They enjoyed the social interaction and the shuttle service to doctor appointments and to the malls. They felt comfortable and familiar in their surroundings. Then they began having serious medical problems. Both they and their family were relieved they had chosen a senior living facility that offered extensive medical care in another wing of the same building.

A widowed neighbor who lived alone moved into an assisted living home at the urging of her children. She dragged her feet all the way. And then after a short time, she told me, "You know, I should have moved here long ago. It's a blessing to be here among so many people. I don't know why I was so stubborn about leaving my home. This place is so much easier, and I have companionship any time I want it."

Appreciate That Reminiscing Is a Precious Gift: It is no accident that God made people so that the older they get the better they remember the good things of long ago and the less they remember the mundane and objectionable things of the present. Long-term memory is far better than short-term memory as most people get older. Dad used to tell me, "I have a good memory. It's just short."

This trait of old age translates into a very precious gift. To yourself—the pleasure of reliving the best times of your life. To your loved ones—passing down the family lore and faith. And to your friends—sharing your life's adventures together.

A professional friend read this book and told me it changed her attitude—the way she approached her aging relatives. She said she always felt her visits were a matter of obligation, enduring the visit rather than enjoying it. The ideas in this book made her realize she could change that by taking charge of the visits and using the time with family members to learn more about their past and her own heritage.

It's easy to lose patience with older people and resent hearing the same stories over and over. I encourage everyone to have your own agenda when spending time with older folks. Ask questions about things you want to know more about. Most older people welcome the chance to tell tales from the past, so if you're tired of the same old stories, ask for new ones. Ask what games they played in their youth and what holidays were most memorable. Find out about their dreams—the ones they fulfilled and the ones not yet met. Ask about their faith journey, their church experiences, and their relationship to God. Remember, you can often get important information about family history, rituals, and values. And be ready to either record or write down what you hear. Every person is like a library . . . a great resource of life experiences and knowledge that should be passed down from generation to generation.

When Dad was ninety-eight, we took our six-year-old grand-daughter, Amanda, to visit him. She sat on his lap and asked me to write out a question for him. "Ask Grampa to draw me a picture of the house he lived in when he was a little boy." They got down on the floor, and with crayons Dad drew a picture of his home in Oregon, Illinois, where he had been born in 1884. Then he drew a picture of his room that he shared with several brothers. He put in the bed and a dresser that was pushed against the wall. Then he gave the crayon to Amanda and said, "Now you draw me a picture of your room with the furniture in it."

Amanda sat very still while she thought about how to draw her room. Then she drew her bed with pictures on the wall and stuffed animals scattered around, and a dresser that was pushed up against her wall. She asked me, "Where did I get that dresser?" I realized her dresser had come from my dad's house, and they both shared the same family heirloom. When I told Dad that Amanda now had his old dresser in her bedroom, he hugged her tight and they both laughed. "It's wonderful to talk about how we are all connected. God has a beautiful plan for all of us."

Reminiscing just may be a God-given tranquilizer for easing you out of this life and into the next.

Good-bying can also be humorous. A religious cowboy, getting ready to say good-bye, made a final arrangement at the nearby tombstone outlet. He described his wishes, paid for the design, and left orders that when he died the monument would be erected on his grave. Since his death, visitors are amused when they stroll past his burial site and discover a statue of Jesus, clad in a long robe, with one foot exposed—wearing a cowboy boot.

SIMPLIFYING THE GOOD-BYING PROCESS

- Resist resistance to change.
- Accept reality.
- Acknowledge that dependency will happen.
- Understand the burden on caretakers.
- Look at options.
- Appreciate that reminiscing is a precious gift.

12

ANTICIPATING YOUR FINAL DAYS

Backing up hills in an old jalopy was not unusual for my brothers. When I was a little kid, Johnny and Bobby bought a black 1921 Model T for seven dollars and rebuilt it. Unlike most cars, that car had more power going in reverse than it did going forward, and Kentucky hills required a lot of backing up. All our family and friends accepted its defects and drawbacks. It looked different from other cars, and less was expected of the Model T because everyone knew it was facing its final days. But that didn't detract from the enjoyment.

Recognizing and accepting limitations—and sometimes that means backing into life's activities—means doing things a bit differently, and not expecting as much from yourself as you would from a younger model. Accept the challenge of adjusting to changes and know that new restrictions will alter the way you live . . . and that you *will* need more assistance.

In addition to the general plans discussed in the previous chapter, you need to think about some specific details concerning arrangements for your final stage of life, which can last a few months or several years. Nikki was sixty-three when she told me she had just been diagnosed with an immunity deficiency disease that would limit her life, both in style and duration. Doctors suspected an earlier blood transfusion was the cause. They informed her that there was no cure for her condition and very little was known to help.

When I asked Nikki about her symptoms, she said there was no pain, and she didn't feel any different, but the doctors told her the disease would cause major problems later on and would shorten her life. Although she knew about her health predicament and did what she could to treat it, she found it difficult to make end-of-life preparations. Thinking that she had a life-threatening illness seemed so unreal. In the seventh year of her final days she developed trouble breathing, walking, and eating. And when the end came, she still had no going-away plans.

In contrast, Greg, forty-one, had a brain tumor and was told he would probably not live until his next birthday, which was three months away. A part of him refused to believe it, but another part, recognizing changes that were already taking place, let him know he was looking at his final days. Sometimes his speech was affected and walking became difficult. Greg decided to use his good days to look at options that would make life easier for his family. He called hospice for information and signed up for their services. He knew he could not pass the required medical exam for long-term care (LTC) insurance, so he set aside a sum of money to help cover the cost of his care. Most significantly, because Greg talked with his family about his concerns and wishes, they were able to maximize every opportunity to pour joy and meaning into his last months. He lived a year beyond his doctor's expectations, but made the most of all the time he had.

WHAT YOU CAN DO ABOUT YOUR FINAL DAYS

If only you could know the timing and circumstances of your final days, as is the case (somewhat) with a pregnancy, then you could prepare more precisely and thoughtfully. The fact that you don't know the exact timing, however, does not mean that you can't plan at all.

Actually there's a lot you can do to make your sunset days much easier for your loved ones as well as yourself.

From my experiences as a therapist, I know that many of you have just begun to allow this term *final days* to enter your vocabulary. You may resist even thinking about the last few "pages" of your "final chapter." Yet you know that time will come for everyone. What can you do?

Accept the Inevitable: You can learn to accept the end-of-life phase as a natural passage that everyone must experience. As a child, you mastered the skills of growing up and becoming independent. Now you may resist being dependent on anyone else. But in your final days, most likely, you will not have a choice. Dependence in some degree will be a necessity. If you can visualize this experience now and accept it as a normal stage in the human journey, you will lessen the trauma of giving up your independence when that time comes. And your ability to be a gracious receiver will make things much easier for whomever your caretaker might be.

My Aunt Daisy was a feisty old lady of eighty-two when she told her three children they had to get ready for the end of her life. They argued with her saying there was no need to think about her dying at this stage. She had lots of years ahead of her, they told her.

Aunt Daisy had always called a spade a spade and she was not about to change now. "You are not being realistic. We all know my days are numbered, so we need to think about what assistance I'll need in the near future. That's just the way life is. I'd like to move into some kind of assisted living while I can still get around and be involved in the decision before I'm too out of it to make the adjustment. If you help me make this transition, it'll be easier on all of us."

Aunt Daisy was ready to accept the reality of her situation, but her children were resistant. Children may think it's compassionate to try to talk their aging parents out of thinking about the end of life, but if they are willing to have open discussions about what's ahead for everyone, it will be easier for all the family to make healthy transitions.

Write Letters of Permission: The dying have to speak of things they have spent a lifetime avoiding, saying the unsayable, going for the big truths—issues surrounding death. You can help your loved ones prepare for your final days by talking about your thoughts and concerns.

Jenks and I have often discussed this topic. What would we want the other person to do if one of us became seriously incapacitated? First we talked about our ideas, then we wrote down our wishes and included them in our Going-Away File.

It sounds something like this: "At the end of my life, when I can no longer care for myself or make rational decisions, I know I will be dependent on you or someone you choose. I want you to know that I give you the freedom to do what you think is best for me, as well as for yourself, and others that are involved. I would like to be cared for in a loving way, but I do not want you to sacrifice your health, your finances, or your relationships. At the end of my life, when I no longer know what I'm saying or doing, I may make unreasonable demands. Right now—while I am in my right mind—I want to say I do not expect you to give up your life for me. Do the best you can to make me comfortable and pain-free. That may mean I will live in an assisted living facility or a nursing home, and that's okay with me. I want hospice to care for me in my final days."

Joe, a family member, recently gave me a letter that he composed after watching a good friend with Alzheimer's disease become an overwhelming burden and embarrassment to family and friends.

> To my spouse, children, and sisters: In light of the various alarms that we have recently witnessed (friends succumbing to Alzheimer's, reports of brain shrinkage causing anger, etc.), I acknowledge the need for personal safeguards. I hereby agree that if any three out of five of you sign this paper and confirm to me in person your concerns, I will address the issues.
>
> Of course, if I'm absolutely bonkers, I'll probably ignore the whole thing. Then someone else will have to take action when I am unable to recognize the need.

Signed_____ Date_____

Dear Joe:

We have noticed new quirks in your nature, changes in your behavior that concern us. We recommend the following steps in detecting, diagnosing, or remedying what we have come to view as a problem with serious implications:

1.

2.

3.

We sign with love,

Date _____

This letter is a beautiful example of insightfulness and a caring gift to his loved ones. You may think of other ways to prepare for your final days and to inform your family about your wishes. Such a document can be one of the most thoughtful ways you can create a loving legacy and prepare for life's major changes.

Consider Long-Term-Care Insurance (LTC): Another option to consider is the purchase of a long-term-care insurance policy, which provides coverage for nursing home care.

An elderly couple sat in my office, discussing their final days with their daughter. They told her stories about when they were responsible for the care and nursing home costs for their aging parents many years ago. Then, with satisfaction gleaming from their faces, they presented their daughter copies of LTC insurance policies they had purchased after their parents' deaths. "When our time comes and we need assisted living, we want you to use these policies to pay for our extended care. That is how we want to take care of ourselves at the end of life. We don't want you to have to go through the same kind of pain and expense we did with our parents in their last months. This is our gift to you."

It has been estimated that roughly 25 percent of people over sixty-five will spend a year or more in a nursing home, and an extended stay in a nursing home can devastate your savings. It is not unusual to pay $3,000 to $5,000 per month. A recent survey shows that the average nursing home resident is underinsured. Medicare pays full benefits for only the first twenty days in a Medicare approved facility and scales back to zero after one hundred days. For information about Medicare benefits, call 1-800-633-4227 and request a booklet called "Medicare and You." It contains much useful information. Medicaid, a welfare program, will cover expenses in some facilities if your income is below a certain level. In Texas income cannot exceed $530 a month. And maximum assets cannot exceed $2,000 for individuals and $3,000 for married couples. Each state has different criteria and the amount changes each year to account for inflation. Call the human resources department or similar agency in your state for more information.

Be Familiar with Hospice: Whether you use hospice or not, you and your family should be familiar with their services. Hospice is the gold standard in end-of-life care and an invaluable resource. "Hospice care is Medicare's hidden treasure," said Iowa Senator Chuck Grassley. "Too few people use the hospice benefit for too little time. That has to change." A coordinated and comprehensive program of care and support for the *terminally* ill and the family, the goals of a hospice program are to allow patients to remain in familiar surroundings (at home, if possible), to be in control of their lives as long as possible, to be pain free, and to die with dignity. Their services are available to people who can no longer benefit from curative treatment. In other words, when treatment by a medical doctor or a hospital cannot save their lives. The typical patient is one who has a life expectancy of six months or less and is referred to hospice by the doctor, nurse, or family. Usually the patient remains at home, or goes to an alternative residence such as a nursing home, assisted living facility, personal care home, or hospital.

The multidisciplinary hospice team includes physicians, nurses, clergy, volunteers, and aides who stand up for the patient. Their objectives are to make a person comfortable, relieve suffering, and help each one maintain a sense of readiness for a "good death." Hospice acknowledges dying as a normal process; they neither hasten nor postpone death. This caring community provides personal care, professional nursing, case management, social services, spiritual counseling, home health aid, volunteers, and bereavement services. The entire family is considered a unit of care, and the hospice focuses on *quality,* not length of life. Medicare, Medicaid, and private insurance are accepted. No one is turned away from services because of inability to pay.

Hospice can be there for the dying, but this incredible organization also offers guidance and support for the family of the patient. One client told me that having hospice around at the end of her mother's life was like having a road map through the final journey. They also acted as a pathfinder *after* her mother's death, giving direction to the family as they navigated the painful grieving phase.

Before considering hospice, do some homework. Weigh the pros and cons of the local hospice programs. Visit several hospices to compare how they operate and to understand what each one does. Ask your clergy or doctor which ones they've had experience with, and talk to people in your church who may have used a hospice program. After you have researched hospice organizations in your area, select the one you prefer to meet your future needs. Write down the full name, address, telephone number, and other pertinent information, and put it in a folder labeled "Hospice" for your Going-Away File.

Questions to ask hospice:
- What services do you furnish?
- How does your program provide pain control?
- Who is on your hospice team and how are they trained?
- What emotional and spiritual support will be offered by trained clergy or mental health professionals?
- What is your track record? How long have you served the community?
- Are you experienced with my illness?
- Does insurance or Medicare cover your charges?
- Do you have a residential facility for patient care?

Hospice can serve as a caring shepherd on your last journey, and can add dignity and peace to life's closure, both for you and your family.

WHAT DO YOU WANT IN YOUR FINAL DAYS?

The most common wants of people in their final days are to be comfortable and free of pain, to be with people they love, to share their stories, to be touched by loved ones, and to feel a sense of peace in safe surroundings.

My ninety-year-old dad didn't have any trouble telling me what he wanted me to do to make him comfortable. "Put that pillow on the porch swing to cushion my bottom. Bring me my pipe and tobacco so I can enjoy a smoke before I nap."

Knowing what you want and asking for whatever provides *comfort* are ways of taking charge of your final days. A woman dying of colon cancer asked her husband to dip a cloth in witch hazel and lay it across her forehead. That is how her mother had comforted her when she was sick as a little girl. A World War II veteran pilot asked to hear the Army Air Corps song as he lay on his deathbed.

My Grampa lived next door to us in his final years. He kept a silver comb and a heavy wooden brush on a table near his favorite chair, so that I, then age four, could fix his hair. I knew it pleased him because he'd shut his eyes, relax, and pat my hand from time to time. I felt very important doing something comforting for him.

Besides physical comfort, most people in their final days want *companionship*. That might mean long visits from those they love or short conversations with a friend or neighbor. I know people who call shut-ins every day to visit and check up on them. It is vital to let others know if visits, phone calls, and companionship would please you. Many people in their final days want a chance to reflect on the past, connect with their families, and *feel at peace* with themselves. They yearn for the people they love to express affection, relate significant stories, and show concern. And the greatest gift is *touch*. Holding a hand, touching a shoulder, rubbing a back, and massaging feet are all ways to make a person feel loved and cared for.

The worst kind of loneliness is to be unable to talk about dying with people you love. One woman told her family, "I don't want to act like I'm not dying. Dying is what I'm doing now. I want to tell you how that feels." Sometimes serious talking is the most powerful therapy.

Ira Byock, M.D., author of *Dying Well,* observed, "When people were allowed to die in comfort around those they loved, dying became an important stage of life."[1] The dying process offers opportunities to complete relationships, review life, and tell one's stories. Sharing stories provides a sense of connection, of leaving something valuable with those you love. And being able to say early good-byes improves mental health.

Meaningful things can be accomplished at the end of life: reconciliation with family members; discovering important perspectives and values; setting real priorities that include expressing appreciation for friendships, the beauty of sunshine in the morning, and forgiveness of self and others. You need to start the process whenever you sense the need, before dementia or Alzheimer's disease affects your ability to communicate lovingly. Since my father lived to be one hundred and had numerous scrapes with death, he had the opportunity to look his final days straight in the eye many times. He told me that he'd practiced dying so often that he ought to be good at it.

While you still have a clear mind, label a folder "Comforting Acts" for your Going-Away File. Put reminders in it, like lists or notes of simple acts of compassion you'd like from your friends, family, and caregivers during your final days. Make sure your family knows about this special folder. When the time comes, fulfilling your own personal wishes will comfort you . . . and them. These comforting acts might include having your hair combed, a foot massage, a backrub, a soft pillow to hold, or listening to special music. For many people in their final days, what gives the most comfort is someone reading the Bible to them. Singing or humming familiar church hymns can provide a sense of peace. And don't forget the power of prayer. In one family, all the relatives gathered around the father's deathbed, held hands, and prayed the Lord's Prayer together.

WHAT DO YOU FEAR?

Experiencing the final journey can be confusing and frustrating. Questions abound: What will happen, how will death come, and what should I do to prepare?

The *unknowns* are scary, like the fear of outliving the money, for instance, and the consequences of that. But there is more to preparing for the final leg of your journey than dollar bills. Dying is a bridge between this life and the next. The question is how to cross that bridge successfully. In the final days, people often wonder if they have done enough good, they are "right with God," and what will happen to them after death. That is understandable. Everyone could have done more, been more loving, lived a better life. (Personally, I'm depending on God's forgiving grace.)

If you are frightened about what will happen to you after your death, call in your minister, or another spiritual leader, or a friend who has a strong faith to talk to you. It is normal to be concerned at the end of life. Talking with your minister about your fears and doubts can help; a pastor can be reassuring and pray with you. You may want to request communion as a final ritual at the end of your life. It can be comforting to call in a special friend with a strong faith, who is familiar with your life experiences, who can remind you of your worth as a child of God.

Most people are not afraid of dying. They fear the *dying process:* the possibility of facing severe, prolonged pain, losing your dignity, or becoming a burden to your family. You may be uncertain about the procedures and wonder, "How will my death look to loved ones? Will there be dignity? Will my final days be something horrible that my family will hold as a last memory of me?" Most people want to "die well," but don't know how to do it.

Talking about your concerns with loved ones and with your spiritual mentors will help reduce the anxiety. Hospice is experienced in handling fears and concerns, and they will manage your pain and help you prepare for the end.

CHOOSING YOUR CAREGIVERS

At the end of life, it is important to trust someone to be in charge of making you comfortable and pain free without taking advantage of you or your resources. You should have someone who will be a good companion, who will be interested in your feelings, who will talk with you about what's happening in your family or neighborhood. And you will need someone who will listen to your stories and memories from the distant past—even if you repeat them often.

If you have family and close friends, take a mental journey past the faces of the people in your life that you love and trust. Write down their names. Then go through your list and mentally note those you would be willing to give legal responsibility for your care. Select from this last list the few people (or the one) that you would like to be in charge of you when you become dependent on others. Pray about the people on this list, then talk to someone you can confide in, such as a clergyperson or a doctor. You're considering putting your life and possessions in the hands of this person; consider your decision carefully.

Now list everything you will need to entrust into their hands: your home, car, checkbook, health care decisions, possessions, pets, obligations, etc. Also list your desires and explore your fears. What do you want to occur in this uncertain situation? What could go wrong? What will it cost? What if something happens to those you depend on? How can you prevent being taken advantage of? What legal forms and agreements are needed?

Next write out a narrative, a plan, of how you would like things to be handled for you when you can no longer make decisions for yourself. The person you select to be in charge of your final days needs written permission to care for you and handle all of your affairs when you are unable to do those things. Put this information in a folder labeled "Caregivers" for your Going-Away File.

I realize that some of you have no family or close friends to turn to for loving and reliable support in your closing days, which makes this dilemma even more frightening. I work with many people who have no close relatives, and they feel isolated, helpless, and vulnerable. However, there are options that you need to consider, many of which could help.

Is there a neighbor that you would feel comfortable asking to help you with this concern? Maybe your minister or someone else in your church could arrange help for your final days. Many denominations have central agencies to address such situations; some also operate assisted living facilities at little or no cost to church members. Your doctor or attorney could be a resource. You might even have to reach far and consider a distant relative who could be in charge of your care. A fraternal organization that you belong to might offer some assistance. And don't forget that hospice can be there for you at the end. Of course, if you have the financial means, you can hire someone to be with you or move into a nursing home where you would receive professional care.

Consider your options and try to make plans for the time in your life when you will need assistance. And the reality is that if they live long enough, all people will reach that stage. Whatever arrangements you make, review your plans on a regular basis, because changes happen. Also, have a backup plan, in case the person you selected is no longer available to care for you.

Our daughter Toby told me that if she could die in her sleep, before she becomes incapacitated, it would be like winning the lottery. Unfortunately, you can't depend on that. But you can anticipate your final days and put together responsible plans that will make your death considerably less chaotic for those you leave behind.

DAD'S FINAL DAYS

In October 1984 our son Rick and his wife, Dede, walked into Pop Little's room at Carmel Manor Nursing Home after traveling a thousand miles from Texas.

"What are you doing here?" Dad asked.

Rick explained, "Your nurse called and asked us to come to see you because you were not doing well. And Margie and Jenks are in Greece."

"Well, I'm sorry the nurse bothered you. There isn't anything you can do for me now. I'm just living out my days here. I'm feeling kind of good for nothing."

Rick wrote, "What else are you feeling? Are you in pain?"

"I hurt all over. My behind hurts. I can't sleep. Food doesn't taste good anymore. My eyes are too dim to read, and I don't even enjoy smoking a cigar."

Dede asked, "What would make you feel better?"

"I wish the doctor would give me something so I wouldn't hurt so much. I ache all over. When I tell him, he doesn't do anything."

That's all Rick needed. He called the doctor and told him his grandfather was in pain and needed relief. "I want you to prescribe stronger medicine so he won't hurt all the time. And I want you to do it today."

The doctor was reluctant, saying anything that strong might shorten his life. Rick chuckled, "But, Doc, my grandfather is over a hundred years old. He's hurting and needs help. There is no excuse for him to be suffering at this point in his life. When will you call in the medicine?"

While they waited, Rick and Dede diverted Pop's attention from his aching body. They asked him questions about his life. "How did you get that job in Beirut, Syria, in 1910? What was it like for you to be in such an unusual place? That was an amazing accomplishment for you. Not many people traveled that far away back then. What did you bring home?"

They had touched some precious memories. My father was eager to talk about his three-year experience in the Middle East. "Getting that appointment to teach at the university in Beirut was a once-in-a-lifetime experience. It has given me wonderful memories that have entertained me during this time when I can no longer read. Yes, that was quite an adventure. Guess the mummy hand was the most memorable thing I brought back from the Holy Land. Has Margie ever told you her stories about that unusual treasure?" He didn't wait for them to shake their heads.

"When Margie was in about the third grade, she invited school friends home to view the mummy hand and charged them each a penny to look at it. Then when she was older, she'd stick that thing under visitors' pillows and scare them to death."

Rick and Dede wondered what had happened to the mummy hand. "I'm sorry to say I gave it to your Uncle Bob and his kids when they were visiting one time. They've never mentioned it again. I imagine it's been lost by now. Wish I'd given it to Margie. She seemed to appreciate it more than anyone."

Dede asked, "What else do you remember about Margie when she was a little girl?"

"Well, Margie was born when her mother was forty-eight years old. Guess you could say she was a surprise. And that about sums it up for most of Margie's life. Always a surprise. Doing the unexpected. Before she could read or write, she was making what she called scrapbooks. She'd sit for hours and cut pictures out of magazines, paste them on paper, punch holes in the pages, tie them together with colored yarn, then give them as gifts. Pictures of cakes, pies, and flowers were in her mother's book. Since she knew I liked to garden, mine had rakes, hoes, and vegetable seed pictures. Her sister, Fran, was a beauty, so her scrapbook contained pictures of glamorous girls wearing pretty clothes and queens with crowns on their heads. Some of our relatives called Margie 'Merry Sunshine' because she was always smiling, happy, and energetic. Margie got her mother's looks and my sense of humor. Good thing it wasn't the other way around."

While talking to Rick and Dede, Dad would sometimes doze off. Then he'd wake up and be ready to talk again. "When Margie was little, she helped me when I sawed logs for the fireplace. She'd get on one end of the bucksaw and we'd saw away. Sometimes she was more of a nuisance than a help. When Margie and Jenks were dating in high school, I thought Jenks was lazy and wouldn't amount to anything. I told her that, but fortunately, she ignored me. Your father turned out to be one of the finest men I know. He's been like a son to me. You know, Rick, you are named after me. Your middle name is Roy, but you always thought you were named after Roy Rogers. You're a go-getter like your mom."

He looked at them closely. "Rick and Dede, thanks for coming to Kentucky."

Rick told me later, "After the medicine arrived, Pop took the pills and began to feel much better. He was eating again and even smoking his cigars. He told us to go back to Texas. He was doing okay."

A few days later Sister Rose went to Dad's room. She stood by his chair while writing out my phone message for him to read. "Margie and Jenks have just returned to Houston from Greece, and they will be here tomorrow to see you." He seemed to go into a trance; his eyes glazed over. Sister Rose told him to go for the light. He nodded his head and died in her arms.

13

I Don't Know What to Say—
I Don't Know What to Do

Where are the cue cards when you need them? Who can tell you what to say to people who are facing death—their own or that of a loved one? You don't get to practice. Communicating anytime is challenging enough, let alone when attempting to talk with the twenty-eight-year-old woman who today got the report that she has systemic lupus, or the eighty-year-old great-grandfather who is dying with colon cancer, or the parents who just received news of their teenage daughter's death in an automobile accident. Feeling inadequate and uncomfortable, you may resist even trying to offer help and comfort.

While I was home from college for Christmas vacation in December 1943, Syd Cornell, sheriff of Southgate, came to our home one evening just after dark with a telegram—outlined in black. The message read *"The U.S. Navy regrets to inform you . . .* (Oh no, no, no) *. . . that Commander John R. Little, U.S. Naval Air Force, USS Yorktown, has been shot down near the Solomon Islands in the South Pacific and is missing in action. The U.S. Navy offers condolences."*

Those words are seared into my mind. My heart still aches from the void left by the loss of my oldest brother, who was twenty-eight years old when his plane went down. Even now, half a century later, I remember being in our living room in a state of disbelief. Standing next to me were Mom, Dad, and John's wife, Voris, who was living with us while he was overseas.

Dad spoke first. "Well, John is missing, but he's a survivor. They don't say he was killed, so we'll just pray he will be found." Mom, Voris, and I cried. Dad scolded us. "Crying won't help. There is no need to waste tears. We will go on with our lives and hope for the best." Anger toward my father stayed with me a long time for his handling of that piercing moment. He was not helpful to any of us with his admonition to stop our grieving. We cried quietly . . . when Dad was not around. My other brother, Bobby, was still fighting the war in the South Pacific and my sister, Fran, was a flight attendant with American Airlines. They heard the news later and did their grieving away from home.

Dad did not want us to talk about Johnny or our sadness. His grieving was internal, isolated from family members, solitary and silent. For many months our house was a joyless tomb. No trace of my brother was ever found, and he was declared dead after a year. My parents held a memorial service at our little Presbyterian church, and a permanent bronze plaque was made with John's name, rank, and "lost in action" engraved on it. On the day of the memorial service, my parents arranged for a blanket of white carnations to hang around the plaque.

Sad years followed for our family. Johnny's death, and the way it was handled, caused a huge rift between my father and the rest of us. Many years passed before Dad found words to talk about my brother's life and death. I know now that he was so devastated over losing his oldest son that he was unable to hear his name or express grief. He did not know what to say or what to do.

Johnny was ten years older than I was, and when we were kids, he was the family prankster. He made us laugh. I was the youngest, the "shrimp" of the family, and he teased me mercilessly. He'd point to my chest and say, "Hey, Shrimper, what's that on your shirt?" I'd look down and he'd tweak my nose. I fell for it every time. When Mom worked at the kitchen sink, he'd come up behind her, push his knees against the back of hers, and catch her as her legs buckled. His Christmas gifts to the family, bought the night before, were put under the tree in drugstore bags.

Johnny made a "lasting impression" on me when I was about four. He was building a pushcart, which was an orange crate on a long board, with roller skate wheels. I wanted to help. He wanted me out of his way. I refused to leave and continued to pester him. Out of frustration, he tapped me on the head with his hammer. He didn't mean to harm me, just get rid of me. I was knocked out and bloody, and he was scared.

That blow deadened the coloring cells and caused a white streak in the front of my hair. Kids called me "the old gray mare" or "the skunk." I tried to cover the white hair with black shoe polish. I cut it off. Nothing ever made it go away. The white streak is still in my hair. Now I like it. Since becoming an adult, many women have asked me what I use to make my streak. When I tell them a hammer, they lose interest.

I wish our family had been able to talk about Johnny's life, his accomplishments, and his death at the time of the tragedy, but that was not the way we coped with crisis. That memory has influenced my philosophy about the importance of sharing feelings and communicating about death.

Years later, Dad and I had many conversations about my brother. He told stories I hadn't heard before . . . about Johnny running away from home as a kid, getting in a fight, spending a night in jail, and writing home from college asking what he could do to be more successful in life. After Johnny's death, my father nailed a metal plaque on the walnut tree in our backyard. It read "In memory of Commander John R. Little, lost in the South Pacific, December 28, 1943, while serving his country as a naval pilot in World War II."

Church members and friends tried to comfort my family, but their words often made our pain worse. Neighbors would say things like, "Just be thankful you have other children. John was serving his country; you must be very proud. God must have needed him in heaven. God is good and will provide." They all meant well but their remarks were not helpful. It is extremely difficult to know how to talk to someone about death. A lot of it has to do with the fact that most people are uncomfortable addressing the subject and are trying to make themselves feel better. And some people spend a lifetime trying to avoid talking about death.

Healing is a long process, and knowing what to do or what to say during this time is often a mystery.

COMFORTING THE DYING

Before I became a therapist, our minister asked me to visit Amy, a church member, who was very sick in the hospital. Maxine, new to the congregation, asked if she could accompany me. She had recently moved to Houston and wanted to get involved in the church. While driving to Methodist Hospital, she asked me about the patient we were going to visit. I didn't know Amy well, but I had served as an elder in the church with her husband, Hank. I had been told that she had cancer and that Amy and Hank had two teenage daughters.

As we entered room 317, I suggested to Maxine that we each pray silently that our words to Amy would be helpful. She was lying in bed, her face ashen. Hank was holding her hand. After introducing ourselves, we said we had come by to see how they were doing. Her husband stood up to greet us and told us our visit was timely. In a halting voice, he said, "Our doctor just left. He told us that Amy's latest MRI shows her cancer has spread. The chemo treatments have not reduced the tumors." He sat down on the bed and sobbed. "The doctor thinks Amy has only a few weeks to live."

I stepped close to the bed and touched Amy's fragile shoulder. "It's painful to let go of life, isn't it? But there is more to us than our physical body." Tears filled her eyes. She nodded, took my hand, and said, "Will you help Hank deal with this? It is so hard on him."

The dying are often more concerned about survivors than they are about themselves. Amy was no exception.

Speaking softly, I asked, "How long have you known about the cancer?" Hank explained that the diagnosis was made a year ago. Quietly, Amy corrected him. "It's been longer than that. Remember the summer we went camping and I had pain and difficulty breathing? The twins were thirteen and now they are fifteen."

I wondered aloud, "What were the girls' reactions when you told them about your cancer?"

Hank answered, "They were sad, but we all thought Amy could beat it. We had a good doctor, and we felt confident that the treatment would cure the cancer, or at least put it in remission. The girls know their mom is very sick, but they aren't aware of this latest news." Tears came to his eyes again. "I don't know how to tell them."

In a cheerful voice, my companion said, "Oh, I think Amy will get better. Don't worry about what the doctors say. They don't know everything. God can heal. Have faith . . ."

I interrupted. "Amy, what do you want Hank to say to the twins? Or would you rather talk to them together?"

Amy tried to sit up, but fell back onto the pillows. "It's so confusing to know what would help. I don't know what to say either. They are good kids. So supportive during all of this. It's agonizing to have to tell them I'm dying. I'll miss their high-school graduations and their weddings. They need a mother. Somehow, I feel I have failed. I won't be here for them." Tears cascaded down her cheeks. "What should I say?"

Sitting on the bed while holding her hand, I said, "It hurts to lose your dreams. The twins have had fifteen years of good mothering. You will be a very special part of them the rest of their lives. Tell the girls how much their support and caring has meant to you. Let them know they are important and that you love them. Tell them of your sadness in leaving them and that dying is hard, but it is a journey we all must take. Remember the good times you have had together. Remind them of God's love and healing power. Encourage them to be kind to each other. And tell them it's okay to cry." Silence filled the room.

I turned to Hank, "What are some of the things you need to do, now that you have this latest information? Have you and Amy ever talked about how you wanted to handle your deaths?"

The engineer side of Hank came through as he began ticking off his thoughts. He mentioned a funeral director that was in our church. "Guess that's where I could begin."

I agreed. "That's a good idea. But, first, you and Amy may want to spend time together, sharing your sadness. Maybe talk about your thoughts and feelings regarding death. Find out what Amy is thinking. Discuss together what you want to say to the twins." Amy leaned toward Hank and said she would like that.

Then she asked me to tell our minister about what the doctor had told them. I assured them I would. I kissed them both, and we left.

Outside their room, Maxine said she was appalled at the way I talked to them about dying. "It was bad enough that they had to hear the news from their doctor. I think you were out of place."

Maxine was using her "Christian" ideas to deny the fact of death—"If you pray and have faith, God will heal you." She missed the Christian belief that a realistic view of death actually affirms our faith—that death is a part of God's plan for each one of us.

Our minister later told me that Maxine reported to him how inappropriate I had been, talking to Hank and Amy about death. He also said that Amy and Hank had related to him how helpful I had been and hoped I would visit again.

FACING A FINAL JOURNEY

How do you talk with someone who is dying? What can you do to help? One of life's most difficult tasks is saying good-bye to a loved one. Feelings are complex. Sadness, helplessness, and fear create confusion. The end of a life is almost always sad, even though death may be a relief for all concerned, especially when physical suffering is involved. Letting go is hard to do.

Since modern culture does not make dying a part of the business of living, death is sometimes seen as alien and unnatural. Contrary to the way it used to be when most people died in their homes, few adults today have ever seen anyone die. Some even refuse to address it. No wonder death feels foreign and is awkward to talk about. Being self-conscious in this situation is normal.

Isabel and Hosea, married twenty-nine years, came to see me because he had an inoperable brain tumor. Isabel blurted out, "Hosea is dying, but he won't talk about his cancer or his approaching death. I get so mad at him."

Hosea turned his head away and looked off into space. Quietly I asked, "Hosea, what are some of the things you don't want to talk about?"

Isabel interrupted, "That's just it . . ."

169

I touched her arm and suggested she listen to Hosea. Again, I questioned, "Hosea, what are the most bewildering things to talk about right now?"

Tears filled his sad eyes. "I don't know where to start. Death is an overwhelming interruption. I don't want to die, and I don't want to talk about it." I put my hand on Hosea's arm and agreed dying is agonizing. When I inquired about his working career, he perked up. As a research chemist, he was exploring new drugs for cancer treatment. Then he said, "It's all so ironic."

I nodded. "You must feel frustrated to leave your project before it's finished."

Hosea looked up and said, "It's like losing my dream of finding a cure for this disease. I have a strong sense of loss . . . of my future. Almost like I'm a failure."

"Do you have any plans for the future journey you are facing now, Hosea?"

In a soft voice he articulated his final chapter. He wanted to be cremated and have his ashes sprinkled in the courtyard surrounding the hospital where he worked. He described the beauty of the rose garden outside his laboratory.

Isabel clicked her fingernails on the arm of the chair, crossed and uncrossed her legs. "How can you tell a stranger all these things and not be willing to talk to me? After all, I am your wife."

Turning to Isabel, I said, "No wonder you feel angry hearing your husband tell me all these things you have worried about. Of course, you're upset. It's not easy to understand why sometimes people find that it's easier to talk with a third party. What else do you want to know?"

When Isabel began to cry, her voice softened. "It's so aggravating not knowing what he's thinking or wanting me to do. I am an organized person, and I simply want to know how to handle all the details about his death. I keep questioning him, but he just ignores me." She sighed.

Hosea reached over and took her hand. "I know you want to help, but you don't give me time to think. You interrupt and ask the same questions over and over. I feel like you are demanding answers. And sometimes, I don't really know what to say."

Touching them both, I spoke, "Isabel, it sounds like you are scared about the future. Losing Hosea is a shock. What do you fear the most about being alone?"

Tears flowed, and I gave her a tissue. "We have been together so long, I can't imagine life without Hosea. He is so important to me. I thought if he could talk to me about his burial and funeral wishes, at least I would be helping him."

In an effort to be helpful, some may come across as overbearing and turn off the ones they love. That happens when they don't know what to say or what to do. Even though I am a therapist and I help people communicate their feelings and work through traumatic situations, there are times when my soul is so full of emotions that the words I speak do not adequately express my feelings. There is sometimes a big gap between what people feel in their hearts and the words that come out of their mouths. Impending death has a way of clouding perspective. Life becomes blurred and communication falters.

Not knowing how to talk about death creates problems for the dying, as well as for surviving family and friends. Those involved often feel pressured, abandoned, and isolated. Or like Hosea—a failure.

Many people handle the subject of death by avoidance. They don't know what to say, so they say nothing or just stay away. After Cody's mother died, he went back to work and to church. People avoided him. Friends who had asked about his mother before her death now backed away from the subject. "I was hoping for support, but instead, they kept their distance." As we talked, Cody realized his friends did not know what to say or what to do. That was probably the reason they avoided him. Just understanding what was going on with them helped him accept the situation, but their distance still hurt.

WAYS TO SHARE YOUR LOVE AND CONCERN

Death ends life, but not its meaning. Asking survivors how they are doing, or just saying you are sorry they have to go through the loss, lets a person know you care. Encouraging family members to talk about the deceased, the funeral, and their feelings can be healing.

When visiting with a seriously ill or dying person, sharing memories is a caring way to communicate. Talking about life's highlights sometimes inspires reflection on past events—what had been important or disappointing. What is left undone—unfilled dreams, loss of the future. At the end of life, there are so many conflicting feelings, more than the heart can hold. Meaningful conversation relieves anxiety. Loving words and actions add so much on both sides. Reminiscing and storytelling reminds them that their life had meaning.

There are other ways to share love and concern for the dying. A young neighbor of a dying client offered to come to his hospital room and play her flute. A ponytailed grandson strummed his guitar while visiting his seriously ill grandmother. Sometimes a foot massage with lotion can be soothing and relaxing. As a kid, I used to give my Aunt Ora a manicure and paint bright red polish on her nails. Afterward, she would put on her fanciest earrings, and we'd watch Lawrence Welk together. When my aging father had trouble walking, we took him in a wheelchair to visit the Cincinnati Conservatory for the Christmas flower display.

Sometimes the best medicine is just being there, and listening carefully. Sit at eye level so the person can see you and your expressions. Let them know that you understand what they say. Repeat key words you hear, nod, and say, "Yes, I see. Tell me more about that." Don't change the subject; let them lead you in the conversation of their choice. Try not to dominate or turn the conversation to what is happening to you. Refrain from giving advice unless you are asked specifically. Then do it softly. Silence is a nonverbal communication and can be helpful. And the gift of touch, like holding a hand and massaging an arm, is very comforting.

When my father, who was ninety-five, stone deaf, and nearly blind, needed cataract surgery, thoughts of him in the hospital concerned me. I sat on the leather footstool next to his favorite chair and wrote to him in big letters, "We need to find a way for us to communicate while you're in the hospital, since you won't be able to see or hear."

Dad agreed. "I wondered about that. But I'll get along somehow."

Being heroic is common behavior for some people; they don't want to cause problems or ask for help.

In big black letters, I wrote, "We'll learn hand signals. When you ask me a question in the hospital, I will squeeze your hand once if the answer is YES. If the answer is NO, I will squeeze your hand twice. You can remember 'No' has two letters, and that means I will squeeze two times. Let's try that with your eyes shut."

He asked, "Will you be with me in the hospital?" I squeezed once. Then he asked, "Will Jenks be there, too?" I squeezed twice. "No," Dad announced. "That works pretty good. Let's practice some more."

I scribbled on the paper. "We'll also want to communicate in other ways. Let's try 'palm printing.'" Dad gave me a quizzical look. I wrote, "I will outline letters in the palm of your hand with my finger, and you spell out the words I am spelling. Let's try it."

He held out his long scraggy hand and closed his eyes. With my finger, I made an *M* in the palm of his hand. Dad said, "W." I realized my printing was upside down to him. So I tried again. I printed out my name, M A R G I E. Dad read "Margie." I squeezed his hand once, saying, "Yes." We laughed together at our new discovery. Then he wanted to try to print in my palm. So it became a game.

We were interrupted by a knock at the door. It was Bill, my childhood friend. He had taken over his family's roofing business after his father died, and he and my dad had become great pals. He often checked the roof of Dad's house and made necessary repairs. Bill told me the last time he put a new roof on the old house, my father was eighty-nine and still wanted a thirty-year guarantee. I explained that Dad was going to have eye surgery, and we were practicing "palm printing." Bill grabbed the pad of paper and wrote, "When you get your eyes fixed, I'll take you to see an X-rated movie." We all laughed at Bill's joke.

In the hospital, after the operation, they wheeled Dad into his room. Bandages covered both eyes. He looked frail and helpless. He lay on the bed, covered with a sheet; his hands were shaking. I reached over, took his hand, and gently made a big *M* in his palm.

Dad held my hand tightly and whispered, "M . . . Margie is here. Everything will be all right." Then he went back to sleep.

The next day, our roofer friend came to see him. Tenderly, he picked up Dad's hand and put a big *X* in his palm.

Dad chuckled. "Bill Grimm, you devil. I'm glad you're here." Dad lived five years after that operation and Bill's palm printing was always a big joke. Humor helps ventilate stress. Laughter softens the letting go process.

SELF-DEFEATING CRITICISM

Talking with the family of the gravely ill can be difficult. There are no right answers, and each situation is different, but criticism is seldom helpful at the time of crisis.

A client told me her husband was seriously ill with lung cancer. She was very upset because when their oldest daughter visited him, she told her father, "You brought it on yourself. I've always told you smoking cigarettes is stupid and would kill you."

Some folks handle their anxiety or grief with unintentional, hurtful, and judgmental remarks because they are angry and feel helpless. Harmful words spring out of their mouths before they can stop them.

Her father told the girl not to visit him anymore. When the mother and daughter returned to my office, the young woman was devastated. She wanted to apologize for her thoughtlessness and ask for forgiveness, but she didn't know how to go about it. She wished she could tell her dad how important he was, and how helpless she felt that she couldn't make him well. I suggested she write a loving note and tell him her feelings.

Before the father died, he forgave her, and they were all together for his final days.

Being diagnosed with a fatal illness causes a variety of reactions among the sick as well as the family and friends. While some folks become verbally judgmental, others criticize themselves and feel guilty about the past. There are those who handle the crisis internally, while grieving the loss of the future. For most, it is beneficial to talk about the pain and the feelings.

When Travis was diagnosed with AIDS, I asked what he was feeling. Shock and disbelief were high on his list. Doctors thought he had less than three months to live, but he had not told anyone about his diagnosis. He relayed his life story to me. Twenty years before, Travis had left his wife and two boys for a relationship with a man. "That was wrong. Now God is punishing me. So I shouldn't be too surprised."

Travis is not alone in his belief. Many people believe that whenever bad things happen, it's because God is punishing them or testing them. I have heard folks say, "I am just being paid back for all the wrong choices I have made in my life" or "I have had such a good life up to now. Now it's my turn to have bad things happen to me."

I don't believe that God makes hurtful things happen to test you or punish you. God loves you and wants the best for each of you, and He provides a path through the valley of the unknown. I believe that God will guide you through whatever happens, and He can give you strength and wisdom to carry on even through the dreadful fog and fear of the unknown.

So I asked Travis about all those other people who get cancer and have not done a "wrong thing."

He sighed relief. "Maybe God didn't cause this condition, but I think I deserve it."

Travis had kept in touch with his ex-wife and children. He had supported them even though they had moved out of state.

Forgiveness began when he told them he was sorry for what he had done. But he still felt too guilty to ask God for forgiveness. I wondered why. He hung his head and said he would sound "like a whiner."

I assured him God could handle it, and that I think there is a whole section in heaven with a sign over it that says, "For Whiners Only." Travis laughed and agreed maybe he wasn't the only one who whines all the time. I asked how he wanted to prepare for his final chapter. He was silent, then said, "I want to be cremated, my ashes spread along the Guadalupe River in the hill country of Texas, where I go camping. I love that area. Then my remains can flow down the river toward Mexico and out into the ocean. Travel is my thing, so that sounds like a good way to go. No telling where I'll end up before I reach the whiners' section in heaven."

UNFINISHED BUSINESS

I asked Travis about other unfinished business. What was left for him to do? When was he going to tell his kids about the diagnosis and his last wishes regarding the spreading of his ashes? After some soul-searching, Travis invited his sons and their wives to visit him. When they all came in together to see me, he had already told them his news. They expressed their sadness and anger at God. Again Travis apologized for leaving them twenty years ago. His children had moved past that event long ago and were now ready to care for and support their father. After visiting the doctor together, Travis and his family spent a long weekend talking about old times, looking at recent pictures of grandchildren he had never seen, and healing old wounds.

When Travis came to see me after his kids left, he spoke of the tears and laughter they had shared together. He felt relieved and proud of his family, their accomplishments, and how they had supported him. I reminded him he had made it happen by being willing to risk calling, inviting them to visit, then sharing his pain. His sense of humor was returning and he was able to laugh at himself. Travis thanked me for helping him verbalize his thoughts and feelings to his family. "By saying 'I'm sorry, thank you, I love you, and good-bye,' our family created a glorious weekend."

Finding the right words can make a big difference when talking to the sick, the dying, and the grieving. See the cue cards on the next page.

CUE CARDS FOR KNOWING WHAT TO SAY AND WHAT TO DO

Just go there. Don't assume someone else will fill the void.	Notice things you can do: cut the grass, wash dishes, bring paper cups, towels, tissues, or a comfort pillow. Run errands.
Encourage talking and reminiscing.	Let them tell their stories—over and over if they want to.
Use the person's name and recall specific events in his life.	Avoid offering advice, unless you are asked.
Avoid clichés and irrelevant conversation.	Ask how they would like to be remembered.
Give a warm hug, hold a hand, touch a shoulder.	Try to keep things as normal as possible. Have a light-hearted touch, when appropriate.
You can't fix it. All you have to say is, "I'm sorry. I wish it were different."	Write an affirming letter. Remind the person of her successes and what she has meant to you.
Avoid using the situation as a springboard to tell your stories.	Allow each one to process the death experience in his own way, no matter how different it may be.
Welcome tears—yours and theirs. Crying is normal and a healthy reaction.	Remember, you don't have to know the answers or solve all the problems.
Avoid judgment and criticism.	Don't take gifts. Just go.

14

What to Do First after a Death Occurs

Nothing ever adequately prepares you for the initial shock of a loved one's death. You are especially unprepared if death occurs without warning, but even if you have been the primary caregiver for months or years, and even if the death relieves you of a great deal of work, stress, and anxiety, nothing fully conditions you for the finality of the death of an important person in your life. Feelings of panic or helplessness may be overwhelming. The emotional impact and the numbness often make it difficult to concentrate on the onerous details associated with what now needs to be done.

WHAT TO DO FIRST

Several things should be done quite soon, but what comes first? If circumstances allow, it can be helpful to spend a few precious moments alone with your deceased loved one. Take some deep breaths and try to bring calmness to your spirit. Say loving, good-bying words. Then if they are involved, call hospice.

If you are the only one present when someone dies, another important thing is to call your pastor, then someone who can be supportive. Maybe a family member, neighbor, good friend, or someone from your church who can provide help and comfort.

Don't worry about waking them. Those close to the deceased and/or the survivors feel included when they are notified about the death immediately. Talking about the death is therapeutic. Saying aloud that a loved one has died can confirm the death in your mind, which is an important first step in the grief process.

If at all possible, have a concerned family member or trusted friend come to your side immediately. You need to have support when making the difficult decisions about removing the body and making all other arrangements. Even if the deceased left behind complete instructions in a Going-Away File, this is an emotional time, and your thinking may be flawed. Perhaps no moment in the death process is as powerful as this symbolic moment of letting go of the body of the person who has died. For these reasons, your family needs to be involved in the decisions about the final disposition of the body. What is most meaningful and appropriate within the family must be determined quickly, and what takes place will be remembered and reprocessed positively or negatively throughout the lives of the survivors.

In some states, a doctor must declare a person dead and verify the cause. If the death is the result of suicide, homicide, or an accident, a call to the county examiner or coroner may be required. If you have been using the assistance of hospice, they will know about these details. If hospice is not involved and you don't know what to do, call 911, tell them why you are calling, and the operator will walk you through the immediate steps you must take.

DECISIONS TO MAKE

If the deceased has not prepared a written going-away plan, decide what you want to do concerning burial *before* calling a funeral home. Your thoughtful decision could avoid excessive charges for services you don't need. For example, if immediate burial is your choice, minimal mortuary services will be involved beyond transporting the body—maybe refrigeration and a low-cost casket. The same is true for immediate cremation, although the cost of a casket could then be eliminated. Under these circumstances, a funeral home with a high administrative fee will be unnecessary.

Once you have called the mortuary, you have time for planning what else should be done. If you know the deceased had prepared a going-away plan, consult it as plans are made.

Remember that as soon as you authorize a funeral home to pick up the body, you may be locked into their "non-declinable" administration fee, which can be exorbitant for what you want. Clarify what you will be committed to and know all the charges. Since there is an additional charge for each service the funeral home provides, you may want to call more than one to compare the cost. (Refer to chapters 8 and 9 for more complete information.) A contract with the mortuary will outline the cost for the functions you request. Funeral and cemetery charge arrangements are usually made in advance, so you should have money available or check to see if credit cards can be used. Be informed about the wide price disparity among funeral homes. You don't have to call the nearest or the fanciest one, or the one your family has always used. You can also ask the funeral home to obtain the death certificates. If an executor has been appointed or if a lawyer is involved, they can also arrange to get them, and usually it is a good idea to get at least six to twelve certificates, depending on the legal needs, such as for banks, brokers, insurance companies, the IRS, etc.

Be sure to stay close to family and friends during this time, and talk about your loss. Expressing your emotions is an important part of the grieving process.

OTHER IMPORTANT CONCERNS

At times, the details will seem endless, but they can also help you get through the first few hours or days, as they occupy your mind. Keep a list of what you've done and need to do, since you might easily overlook details that are not of immediate concern. For instance, check on death benefits to survivors from life and casualty insurance policies, military service, credit union, employer, Social Security, and other sources. These benefits are sometimes overlooked because no one knows about them.

Security is another factor to keep in mind. It is sad that obituary notices sometimes attract crooks. The home of the deceased is sometimes broken into during the funeral service. Many people realize this situation and arrange to have someone stay in the home during that time. When my father-in-law died, the family left the house furnished, hoping to sell it quickly. Thieves broke into the homestead and stole almost everything of value, even the beveled glass in the front door.

Survivors can also expect unsolicited calls from both legitimate sales people and scam artists who make special offers at this time. Survivors are particularly vulnerable and may be tempted to accept what seem like good offers to repair something, like the roof, when in reality, crooks will abscond with an advance payment "for materials" or do a shoddy job. I have also known of situations where two strangers visit the home of the deceased with an offer to help out the survivor or "check up on the utility service." While one diverts the attention of the homeowner, the other is removing items from the house. Do not allow strangers to come into your home. For any legitimate needs you have, stick with your regular tradespeople or consult with friends for referrals.

THINGS TO DO AFTER DEATH OCCURS

This list can be reassuring, reminding you of those necessary actions that must be considered at a trying time—when orderly thinking is often scrambled like a box of jigsaw puzzle pieces.

1. If hospice has been involved, call them first.
2. Call clergy for comfort, planning services, and putting a notice in church papers.
3. Call a family member or trusted friend immediately to help you through the decision-making process regarding the burial and funeral service.
4. Check for any written instructions or information prepared by the deceased that would guide you in determining body disposition, funeral plans, and other details.
5. Call the mortuary to arrange for body disposition, either burial or cremation.
6. Remove jewelry from body.
7. Arrange for verification of death and secure six to twelve death certificates. The funeral home can provide these services.
8. Notify executor, employer, lawyer, CPA, insurance agent, etc.
9. Review insurance policies, including Social Security, employee benefits, credit union, military, etc. for death benefits.
10. List people, including friends, neighbors, colleagues, and out-of-town folks to notify by phone, fax, e-mail, or letter.
11. Plan funeral/memorial service and contact those involved.
12. Prepare obituary, giving time and place of service; decide and list appropriate memorials—charity, church, library, etc. Deliver obituary in person or fax to newspaper.

13. Arrange for childcare or pet care if necessary.
14. Consider household needs such as house cleaning, bill paying, etc.
15. Make arrangements for out-of-town relatives and friends.
16. If deceased was living alone, notify utilities and the landlord, and give the post office a forwarding address.
17. Take precaution against thieves, especially during the time of the service. And ignore unsolicited sales calls.
18. Stay close to family and friends for support.

15

HOPE FOR SURVIVORS

As the youngest kid in our family of six, I played the role of "caretaker of family togetherness." I was in charge of keeping everybody happy, even though family death was also in my thoughts. I prayed that when the time came, our whole family could die together ... so no one would have to grieve. The thought of losing any one of us was more than I could bear. I worried about how death could come for my family, all at the same time—without hurting. Dying by fire was not a good choice. What about lightning striking our house ... and we all wake up dead? Since we didn't have a car, dying in a wreck did not come to mind. Death was a dilemma. There didn't seem to be a good choice for us to die together. So I gave up on that idea. Do you remember any such childhood concerns?

It is not unusual for children to worry about the death of a parent or sibling when there is no apparent reason for such thoughts.

When my two older teenage brothers left the house in the rain to go on a planned Sea Scout outing on the Ohio River, I stood by the window and cried, afraid they might drown. Dad scolded me, "Stop blubbering. Crying won't help anything. Save your worry for sometime important."

As an advanced worrier, I was sometimes a bother to those

around me. I don't know when I decided to give up the job of being in charge of my family's life and death, but at some point, I let go of that obligation. Guess that was when I grew up and got a life.

However, the fear of death is common at all ages and for good reasons. Life is full of uncertainties. Learning to cope with actual loss, grief, and transitions is included in life's most difficult and profound lessons. Even going off to kindergarten is a loss for both mother and child. Losing, leaving, or letting go is how people learn to grow. Mourning is the process of adapting to the inevitable losses that occur in every life.

Sooner or later you are going to face the issue of your own death. But you will also have to deal with the death of a loved one—and most people are usually unprepared for the reactions to such a loss. Often three or four months of depression will follow. You will feel empty, lost, and out of control. Normalcy seems out of reach, impossible to recover. Hardly ever do normal coping skills adequately prepare someone for this kind of fallout. You may become more aware of your own mortality and vulnerability. Fear and emotional involvement with the finality of any severe loss can be the setup for some strange behavior.

When Kent's golfing buddy died suddenly from a heart attack, Kent gave away his treasured golf clubs. He didn't think he could ever play golf again. When Luanne's son was killed in an auto accident, she refused to allow her other children to drive a car.

If you feel the need to take such drastic actions, be aware that it's a normal reaction to grief—one of many you may have in the weeks following a loss.

STAGES OF GRIEF

A cruel loss triggers several stages of grief. The sequence may be different, and grief stages are not always distinct from one another and can merge together. But everyone goes through a coping struggle, and understanding the grief process will help you realize that most feelings and sensations are part of the normal passage toward reclaiming hope for the future.[1] The start of healing is evident when you can get back into the routine of life, doing what needs to be done, and taking care of practical and emotional matters that need attention.

FIRST STAGE: KICK IN THE BELLY

In the "kick in the belly" stage, you will feel like the air has been knocked out of you. Shock, numbness, and a sense of disbelief are the initial feelings. There is an inability to wrap your mind around what you are experiencing. "This can't be happening to me. I will wake up from a nightmare and discover it is all a bad dream." Breathing may be difficult. There is intense psychic pain, disorientation, and an implosion of helplessness.

When my brother John was missing in action during World War II, Mom refused to accept the possibility that he might be gone forever. With eyes riveted on the screen, she watched black-and-white Pathe-News coverage in movie theaters, searching for signs of her oldest son in the war activities in foreign islands. Surely, every ring of the phone would bring news of John's safety. Delayed letters, written before his death, arrived home after he was reported missing. His writings told of combats in unheard of places like Guadalcanal, Iwo Jima, and Okinawa. Couldn't those letters be proof that he was still alive? Death is one of those events that, even when we acknowledged it with our brains, our hearts didn't want to believe.

A year passed. A second telegram declared my brother dead. Hope faltered. The search ended. This second staggering blow immobilized my family. Even putting food on the table was difficult. Family conversation stopped. For me, even getting out of bed to go to school seemed almost impossible. We all felt out of control, hopeless, and isolated. It was a lonely time.

All the people affected by the Columbine High School killings went through this "kick in the belly" stage. That horrible event set off a mourning that tore at the heartstrings of the entire nation. Feelings of disbelief, helplessness, anger, and sadness filled the souls of millions.

We watched those Colorado families and classmates hugging, trying to comfort each other, borrowing strength and stability from one another. They were looking for a pillar of strength, a backboard to lean against and safely bounce off their emerging emotions. A person experiencing this "kick in the belly" stage of grief needs to stay close to someone for support and to be able to cry. There is healing power in tears, a washing away of some of the hurt.

The tragic event of September 11, 2001, had an even more devastating effect, not only on the United States but on the whole world. No one escaped the trauma, fear, helplessness, and anger at the dastardly deeds that crashed into homes around the world by repeated television coverage. People flocked to churches to pray together, hold each other close, trying to console one another, trying to find comfort in their faith. They wanted to feel safe in the arms of a loving God. As questions arose about how God could allow such a thing, pastors, social workers, and grief counselors reached out to help soothe the pain in the belly. Anxiety clutched at the hearts of the observers, fearing what could happen next. The kick in the belly feeling just wouldn't go away. A year later, many of those touched by that tragedy are still reeling from that event, still relying on their faith to get them through the day-to-day events in their lives.

Some people are in so much shock after experiencing a death that they deny their feelings and continue to grieve years later. Delayed grief is common and should be recognized so it can be addressed.

During high school our younger son, Bob, lost five classmates. One boy hanged himself, another died in a car wreck, a girl died of leukemia, a football buddy died on the practice field, and one child drowned. Many years after those events, Bob told me how tough it had been, and that no one at the school ever talked to the class about any of those deaths. He went to the funerals with his friends, then everybody acted like life was normal. But it didn't feel normal to him.

I now realize that I didn't do much to help him. What was I thinking? Even having gone through what I did with my brother John's death, I only attended the funerals of Bob's friends and talked with the families, but I didn't discuss my feelings with Bob nor listen to his. Looking back at his high-school years, our son remembers the trauma he felt, but he never discussed it with anyone. I wish I had been wiser and more sensitive to him and his feelings. Delayed grief prolongs the pain. Grief work is the school people are automatically enrolled in after a death—then they strive to graduate to the next stage of life.

Helping someone move through the "kick in the belly" stage can begin by just *being there and listening*. Encourage a grieving person to express any thought that comes to mind, no matter how irrational it may sound. Being logical in this stage may not be possible or useful. Family and friends can provide a gentle sense of reality. That may be in the form of something as normal as a cup of chicken soup, hot tea, or the gift of prayer. Being there and staying close are some of the loving blessings you can give.

SECOND STAGE: RUNNING FOR COVER

In the "running for cover" stage, the bereaved is searching for an escape—a safe place to hide and get away from the awful truth. Excessive diversion is also common—staying overly busy, frantically cleaning, or making numerous "to do" notes. For some, this is the time when they stay in bed with the sheets pulled over their heads, refusing to get up or leave the house.

In this stage, people are looking for ways to reduce the pain and find something they can control or change so they will feel more in charge of their lives. Unfortunately, the mourning process can go awry. Andy cared for his terminally ill mother, and when she died, he wanted a change. He quit his job, got a divorce, and moved out of the state—much too soon for his own good, compounding his losses. There are those who seek relief in destructive ways, running in the wrong direction to alcohol, illegal drugs, promiscuity, or even suicide.

When I first talked with Betty, I learned that she refused to change anything in the home after her husband died. His clothes still hung in the closet. Next to the ashtray, pipes were lined up in the holder. Almost every object that he once possessed was still in place. She was running for cover by hiding in her husband's belongings. She thought she was honoring his memory. I asked when her husband died. She told me, "Eleven years ago this month." She had created a shrine. A mummification. She was burying herself with her dead husband, living a crippled life, and staying stuck in the moment of grief. At the time of a loved one's death, everyone has choices—one way or another, to die with them or to live. Betty had chosen "the other way," to die while living.

Someone in the "running for cover" stage needs security and stability. Sitting quietly in a church chapel with a friend can be comforting. Staying with a grieving person in their home, or inviting them to yours can provide a safe harbor. The goal is to help them find a "cover" to run to that is reassuring and nurturing, rather than destructive and suffocating.

When my sister-in-law lost her husband after a long illness, we invited her to Houston to stay for a while. She brought some unfinished business with her, including a lot of financial information to sort through. My husband is her only brother, and her visit let them create a special bonding experience. We all talked of past times we had shared with her family. We spoke of her husband's special qualities and how much we loved and appreciated him. Together we thanked God for the special gifts he had shared with us all. Coming to Houston was a great diversion and a safe cover for Jenks's sister. She went home feeling comforted, more organized, and in control.

THIRD STAGE: KICKING BACK—GETTING EVEN

Anger and wanting revenge surface in the "kicking back" stage. Questions that come are "Who can I blame? Who did this terrible thing to me? How can I get even? How can I make someone else hurt as much as I am hurting? Where is God?" In this stage, praying can sometimes be difficult; it is easy to feel alienated from God. Migraine headaches, rapid heartbeat, and stiff muscles can result from extreme stress put on the body. Violent thoughts and strange or irrational behavior may follow, looking for a scapegoat. A common reaction is to clump people together in a category and then hate them all. Classifications may include race, culture, profession, religion, gays, or whatever seems to fit.

A mother whose child was killed by a truck found herself hating all truckdrivers, until her son became a driver for UPS and she made peace with her illogical opinion. When my brother was killed in the South Pacific, I hated all Japanese people, until I met Yoko, a lovable Japanese girl who told me American soldiers had killed her parents. As a part of our healing, Yoko and I attended a church service together and held hands as we prayed for reconciliation among people of different cultures.

Then there was Rodney, who sat in my office with clenched fists. He had just buried his young wife, who had died from colon cancer. He was angry with God, the doctors, and his wife for not seeing the doctor sooner. "She didn't deserve to die," he said through tight lips. "I am so mad at the world I don't know what to do. I want to take it out on somebody. Punch 'em a good one. But I don't know who to go after."

Kacie Jenkins, our fourteen-year-old granddaughter, was so affected by the Columbine High School killings that she wrote a letter to the editor of a California paper reflecting her grief. Her letter was an effort to kick back at some people she considered to be responsible for the deaths at Columbine:

> I am sick to my stomach. This Colorado incident is so incredibly frightening, appalling and devastating. I want to crawl into a secluded corner, and hide from the world and all its terrors.
>
> Constant exposure to violence is the key issue here. The entertainment industry definitely promotes violence. I cannot recall a single movie I have seen this year that did not include violence. Oh, and our music is jam-packed with foul words, threats, telling us to mow people down with machine guns if they don't think the way we do.
>
> I was disgusted to find this morning that I had become numb to the terrible lyrics in rap songs. I listened closely to the words in a Notorious B.I.G. song ("I hate y'all, too, while your gun's raisin', mine is blazin,'") and was horrified.
>
> —Kacie Jenkins

As Kacie discovered, taming the "kicking back" stage is helped if you talk out your feelings or write down your thoughts without being told that you are wrong to feel the way you do. It is a relief to let out your anger. Listening to people who are grieving and agreeing that their feelings are normal can provide support to someone who is fighting back. Let them know they can shout at God. Even write Him a nasty letter. God has very broad shoulders and can handle their anger.

FOURTH STAGE: IF ONLY . . .

Regrets surface in the "if only" stage. If only . . . I had been there, listened more, not given her a car for graduation, said, "I love you" more often. In this stage you can become fragile and take the blame, believing a death or accident was your fault. The result is a high degree of guilt, bringing on depression and sadness; and a belief that you are a bad person, even feeling you have been irresponsible, despite your knowledge that this is not the case. Heart and mind aren't always on the same page when you are grieving.

Patricia told me, many years after her teenage daughter's suicide, that after much prayer and healing, she was beginning to feel relief that she could finally say her daughter's name without guilt. Then added quickly, "But now I am horrified that I *can* say her name without guilt. To give up the grief and guilt seems like a betrayal. I continue to feel I should have been more aware of the signs of depression and done something to save my daughter from killing herself."

These are all normal reactions after the death of someone you love. You want answers that aren't there. For healing to happen, it is necessary to remember that you are *not* able to control all the events in the lives of your loved ones. You can't even control everything in your own life. It is important to accept that you are doing the best you can. And if you did mess up, then it is time to forgive yourself, accept what can't be changed, and move on. Not easy to do, but holding on to irrational guilt is self-defeating. Staying in the "if only" stage will rob you of energy and spirit that you need to build bridges to your future.

The death of a loved one feels like the end of the line. Although life goes on, it takes on a totally different perspective; recovery begins when you acknowledge that bad things do happen to good people. It is not your fault.

FIFTH STAGE: HEALING AND BOOMERANGS

Healing is a perpetual, though irregular, process that begins when you can accept the reality of a loved one's death and realize what that loss means to your future. You can't rush this "healing" stage. There will be days when you think you are okay, then find yourself boomeranging to earlier stages. The goal is to look at the breadth and the depth of life. As time passes, when remembering a tragedy, don't dwell only on the devastating event. One couple told me, "Our daughter lived for thirty-one years. She died on only one day. We want to remember the happy times we shared together and not focus on the one day she died." You know that healing has begun when you are looking ahead to the future and taking some positive actions. Don't be discouraged when total healing is not immediate. It won't be.

Gilbert was thirty-five when his mother died. His understanding boss told him to remember the 3-3-3 process. Then he explained, "The first three days you are numb. Don't even try to do anything. The next three weeks you become aware of what has happened, and the feelings rise. It could take three months, or even three years, to begin to feel normal again."

There are those who believe "you should *just get over it and go*

196

back to work." That philosophy might work for a few people who find therapy in doing something familiar. But usually the bereaved are not able to concentrate . . . for some time . . . after losing a significant other. The mind can play tricks, and mistakes and accidents can happen.

Some people don't know how to grieve, or even recognize that they are going through the agonizing process of letting go. Cindy's husband's death boomeranged on her for ten years after he was buried. She suffered a deep depression, especially on holidays. Each year she remembered the day of his death by staying in bed, feeling sorry for herself, and ignoring invitations from family and friends. Then she complained that nobody cared about her since her husband died.

Resilience is essentially a spiritual issue. Prayer and giving thanks for the time spent with the deceased can hasten the healing process. Sometimes God works at a different pace than you hoped for, but remember: He is a loving God who wants the best for you. Know that, with His help, you can move forward to reinvent your life. It will be an unfamiliar shape from what you had before, but your life can reflect a trust in God. You can celebrate your loved one's memory by reclaiming your power and determination to create a life that honors the one you lost. It is never easy, and it will not be a steady progress.

Parents of a teenager who had died in a tragic accident while driving home from college remembered their daughter with a small memory tree. They set it up in their home and decorated the tree with pictures and mementos from her life. They included letters from friends and snapshots of past shared events. They told me they even got satisfaction from talking to their daughter's picture. The tree was a symbol of her life.

Memory books and photo albums are some other ways to

remember those who have died. One family created a quilt, piecing together patches of embroidered symbols from their son's life. In your grief, don't erase the treasured history. On the anniversary of a death, celebrate the life of your loved one. Do something positive: make a donation in his or her honor or plant a tree or discover a way to pamper yourself, whatever that would mean to you. And don't forget to stay close to God in prayer.

This healing stage is the beginning of a healthy transition. After acknowledging the agony, enduring the pain, experiencing the boomerangs, and surviving it *all*, at some point you will be able to accept the reality of the tragedy that invaded your life. Slowly, almost imperceptibly, your grief will lose its domination, and you will begin to create a new life. It takes longer than you want, but it is possible.

If you deny grief, or attempt to cut it off before the process is completed, it will often go underground, only to resurface in destructive ways: serious depression, isolation, broken relationships, or alcoholism. Don't shut off the anguish. You need to live through it and learn to manage it. Grief is a natural process, like a slow recovery from a serious illness, but piece by piece, you *will* reenter the world.

The fact is that each loss is different in intensity and recovery. Reactions vary. There is not one right passageway through grief. What is important to know is that there are many normal reactions to death. If you can view life's ending as an adventure and talk freely to loved ones, the grieving process will be made easier.

SIXTH STAGE: REACHING FOR NORMALCY

The death of a loved one alters the lives of survivors forever. The effects are so devastating and irreversible that normalcy seems to be permanently forfeited. And, indeed, if *normalcy* means a return to life exactly as it was before the loss, then it *is* gone forever.

The bad news is the *old normalcy* will never return. The good news is there can be a *new normalcy* that accommodates a return to a healthy, productive, and even joyous life.

Normalcy does *not* mean forgetting your lost loved ones. You will hold them in your memory all of your life. Normalcy does *not* mean that all your grief is over. Sadness and heartache will invade your thinking at unexpected times and places. Normalcy does *not* mean that your loved one can be replaced. Each life is a God original—significant and unique. No one will be exactly like the one you lost.

Normalcy *does* mean that your life is no longer dominated by grief. Though it is never totally dissipated, you manage your grief; it does not manage you. Normalcy *does* mean you have survived with your other important relationships intact and you will cherish your connections to them. And normalcy *does* mean that you are pursuing healthy aspirations in life. You will experience new beginnings and discover uncharted pathways.

The loss of a child, for instance, can precariously affect the relationship between the parents. Instead of comforting a spouse, some parents blame or avoid each other and their surviving children. They fail to see that they are cheating themselves and not really honoring the deceased. The healing way through this passage is to support one another, reinvent life, and initiate new designs for living. Redirect energy into satisfying activities and discover interests that deserve your attention. Make sure you are nourishing relationships and not putting death ahead of relating to the living. Try to remain plugged into life by staying in touch with people you love and trust. Success is in the making when loved ones who have supported each other through the crises and the grief are enjoying a newly created life on the far side of tragedy.

After the death of a loved one, everything feels different and unfamiliar, and the search for normalcy becomes a major objective. The problem is, you don't know what the new "normal" is supposed to be. You have not been in this place before, and because you are so obviously at loose ends, dogmatic problem-solvers may come at you from all sides—a relative, a friend, a church member, a neighbor, or a colleague. Each one knows exactly what you should do to "get back to normal." But, in real life, because people are so different and come from such varied family and cultural experiences, there are no "one-size-fits-all" solutions. As experienced as I am in counseling clients through the grief process, I can't write the exact formula for *you* at your particular place in life. This is your own path.

However, looking over a list of "healing behaviors" might help you deal with your loss and reach for your own new normalcy. Read through them and see which ones you can make the most of in your "return to the land of the living."

- *Clarify and reconfirm your spiritual faith.* Draw strength from Scripture, poems, readings, music, and grief support groups.
- *Maintain relationships that will contribute to a successful passage into the future.* The strongest defense against trauma is having good friends and diversified interests.
- *Take time for memories and honor the endings.* Focus on those treasured traits, the good times, and the companionship. Then give your loved ones back to God and have faith that a heavenly Father is waiting to welcome them home.
- *Write about your feelings and share your thoughts.* Some clients tell me they have benefited from writing letters to the deceased.

- *Write about your own private grief journey, your wishes, hurts, and future plans.*
- *Be kind to yourself.*
- *Reconnect with an interest you enjoyed before your loss,* like gardening, athletics, playing the piano, bridge, or doing crossword puzzles.
- *Develop a list of places you want to go and invite friends you'd like to nurture to go with you.*
- *Remember how you cared for your deceased loved one and what you did to make the end of that precious life more peaceful.* It can be a loving gift to yourself.
- *Let your family and friends know how much you appreciate them.*
- *Find humor in each day;* laughing is healing for the soul.
- *Say "I love you" more often* and recognize the love messages that come your way.

And remember, it's okay to be happy again. You never know when a new loss will happen in your life, so learn to live each day as bodaciously as you can. Care about others, and have a passion for life. Live the best you can with grace and gusto. That is the very best way to honor your loved one.

SOME IDEAS FOR HONORING A LOVED ONE
WHO HAS DIED

- Sit by the burial site and reminisce.
- Plant a tree or a garden.
- Donate to a favorite charity.
- Write a poem about your feelings.
- Establish a scholarship.

- Dedicate a bench in the park.
- Write a life-journal about the person.
- Create a memory book of pictures, thoughts, and feelings about your loved one.

16

LIVING BODACIOUSLY WITH GRACE AND GUSTO

Fifty-eight-year-old Alex attended one of my seminars at the insistence of his wife. He told the group that he had spent a year planning for a trip down the Amazon with three friends, then took three months planning a motorcycle trip to the Ozarks with a buddy. "But what is there to plan about dying?" he asked. "You dread it, then you die. That's pretty well it."

A year later, I saw Alex in church and he surprised me by saying, "Your seminar was a real eyeopener. I followed your plan. My Going-Away File is called My Final Expedition, which made me think about some expeditions I *wanted* to take. After discussing it with my wife and kids, I planned a family gathering in Yosemite Park. I took the whole gang: my wife, my eighty-two-year-old mom, our kids, and two-year-old grandson. Fifteen of us. Talk about planning. Developing my end-of-my-life strategy was a heck of a lot easier than coordinating the schedules for that bunch."

Sometimes, getting a grip on the final stages of life can mean learning to live with more gusto *now*. Doors can open that you didn't even realize were shut.

Zola's retired husband died suddenly from a heart attack. Her neighbors and bridge partners, Jordan and Karen, were there to help her through the grief. Two years later, Karen died. Zola and Jordan consoled each other and formed close bonds, built on a long friendship. They talked openly about their spouses and remembered the many experiences they had shared. They grieved. They laughed and cried together. After a year, they married in their church, and a new life of joy emerged from their loss and grief.

I suggested often in previous pages that both the process and the accomplishment of preparing your going-away plan stimulates a profound sense of freedom, a release to live your life to the fullest during whatever time you have left: release from fear of the unknown, release from guilt about things undone, release to use your time for things other than worry, release to pursue your dreams, release to celebrate the gift of the rest of your life.

Of course, you don't totally get rid of everything; there still are some things incomplete, but this release to live boldly after completing your exit plan or surviving a severe personal loss is what I call *bodacious* living. I love this word! It seems to have evolved as a Southern provincialism combining the words *bold* and *audacious* and the *American Heritage Dictionary* says it means "daring, spirited, and original." And that's the kind of living you can experience after you have dealt head on with the business of death.

But it doesn't happen automatically. You must take the "release" that comes with your accomplishments and optimize it—live bodaciously.

Celebrating life multiplies joy—and it's good for your health. You don't have to change a lot to do it. The question is how?

What have you done for fun lately?

When I ask clients this question, they invariably pause and say,

"Nothing." One couple said, "We're too busy, too stressed, too overworked, and too stretched out on credit cards to think about having fun."

Everyone tends to get bogged down in the ordinary, daily routine of life. Some even find comfort in sameness, and don't want to think about adding new dimensions to their existence. And that's fine for some people. Others get bored, crave change, and feel frustrated, but will not try anything new for a variety of reasons. For those of you who want to expand horizons, increase opportunities, and maximize individual talents—congratulations! There are a lot of ways to boost a leg over those fences that confine you.

You have the power to climb over the barriers that prevent you from enjoying a well-lived life, replacing obstacles with constructive actions. Doing the same thing in the same way can become such a habit that you don't think about other ways of living. A client told me about her young son, Mark, who had a pet goldfish in a small bowl in his room. One day Mark decided to clean the fishbowl, so he put his pet in the bathtub with lots of water. Mark called to his mother. "Look at this. My fish goes around and around in a small circle, just like he did in his bowl. He doesn't know he can swim in a larger circle." Without realizing it, some people resist expanding their circles, even when they have the opportunity.

Self-imposed boundaries can create formidable barricades rather than healthy challenges. For example, you may start assuming that you know what others are feeling or thinking. Or you play the "Yes, but . . ." game. You find yourself using the excuse "That's just the way I am." Believing success is made up of giant steps instead of a series of small ones can stop you before you get started. A sixty-eight-year-old marathoner once said, "Running is not hard. Left foot, right foot, left . . ." Energized living starts that way.

I want to encourage you to believe in yourself. Love yourself. Be more bodacious and hold a better self-image in your heart. Stop rejecting compliments that emphasize your positive characteristics. Decide now to see the good things in yourself.

A client sent me a card with a picture of a kitten looking in the mirror. When I opened the card, there was a big powerful lion looking back at me. Written on the inside were these words: "Thanks for helping me see myself as more powerful than I realized."

Create a new habit of focusing on possibilities. There is a lot to appreciate about you. Nurture the habit of counting your blessings each day and seeing yourself as an extraordinary creation of God.

BE YOUR OWN GENIE

Remember Aladdin and his magic lamp? When he rubbed the lamp, a genie popped out and granted three wishes. Amazingly, you have the power to uncork yourself and be your own genie. You have the ability to produce change in the ways you respond to life. To risk is to have hope in tomorrow. Changing your attitude can revitalize your life. Did you know that when indoor toilets were first introduced, many people refused to accept such a ridiculous idea?

Why do you hesitate to be curious about new ideas? What would unlock you from a status-quo life?

YOU MUST WANT TO CHANGE

You have to really *want* to change! Just wishing and hoping won't do it. It takes three things to change: (1) you have to want to;

(2) you have to be very uncomfortable with the way things are; and (3) you have to be open to options that can improve your life—and apply them.

Often, talking to a friend, a family member, your minister, or a therapist can assist you in sorting out changes that will enrich your life. When you are willing to change, the vast realm of ready possibilities will amaze you.

Like the seasons of the year, when God provides beauty and blessing with every change, you can create changes in your life that increase joy and satisfaction. Make God a partner in the process of your reformation. You can add spice and color to your routine by looking at available options and choosing the best ones for you.

⁓

In the early 1970s, when I was fifty-one, I applied for graduate school because I was ready for a change in my life. I had to be willing to give up weekly tennis games, getting together with friends, and volunteering at the church. But after applying, I was told I was too old, that at my age I didn't have enough to contribute, and that they had to fill the spaces with younger, minority, and more adaptive students.

I got angry and asked for an interview, only to be informed that they usually did not grant interviews. I told them people my age usually did not apply. I persisted until they agreed to let me talk with an admissions counselor. After a twenty-minute interview, he announced, "Well, Mrs. Jenkins, this next class does need a chronologically mature white female, and you might fit the bill." So I became the school's "token little old white lady," and my life was changed forever.

A good start in multiplying joy is to gather as many ideas as you can that encourage new adventures and refuse to play the game, "I'll be happy when . . . I have more money, or more time, or when the kids grow up." Instead of waiting for life to begin, celebrate who you are and what you have. Map out an action plan to take yourself where you want to go. What's the first step? Making a phone call? Taking a computer class? Saving for a special happening?

Action leads to a positive mood and valuable self-actualization. Reward your effort. Never stop dreaming. Dreaming is the spark to imagination and accomplishment, enabling you to exceed your expectations.

My friend Clark, a twenty-eight-year-old leukemia patient, dreamed the impossible. In my office, we planned, and he later completed, a solo cross-country bicycle trip. Tied onto his bike were a bedroll, bags of oatmeal, pasta, dried fruit, a stove, a New Testament, a hymnal, and an ice thermos to hold the medication for his daily injections. It was not easy—biking, camping, and medicating his way from Texas to California on an extremely low budget. But his apartment had become a prison, and he wanted a challenge—a sense of accomplishment. Since completing that adventure, his world has expanded. He was interviewed on the radio, spoke at the Cancer Counseling, Inc. (CCI) luncheon in Houston, and had his picture in the paper. He did the unthinkable. A bodacious undertaking.

Accomplish your long-term goals by acting on the numerous short-term opportunities that are all around you. Do something different . . . walk in new places, call an old friend, read a fun book, attend worship services in a different place. Develop deep appreciation for the gifts of life that have been given to you. Express it.

Write a note to a teacher, a friend, or a family member to say how much you appreciate him or her. Ask yourself, "How would my love help?" Then give it away—to those who would most benefit from it. Little things count big. Kindness carries world-shaping power.

BE AN OPPORTUNIST

Invite others to explore with you, and take advantage of every promising possibility. Accept invitations that add spice, but don't exhaust your energy. Be selective. Learn to say "no" to what is not rewarding. It's great therapy.

Instead of being critical or judgmental, develop caring communication. Ask more loving questions. Instead of asking, "Why did you quit?" or saying, "That was a dumb thing to do," reframe your inquiry: "Tell me more about what was going on. What were some problems you were having? How can I help?" Criticism scares the world. Give yourself permission to *not* know all the answers; you don't have to fix everything. Discover the stimulation of respecting opinions that differ from yours. Be tactfully curious. You will learn a lot. Explore new possibilities. If you feel locked inside a prison cell, remember, you hold the key. Live your life with gusto. No one else will.

You don't have to get your name in the newspaper, be an officer in a club, or be inducted into a hall of fame in order to expand your visions or create a new skyline. Look at family, neighbors, coaches, teachers, religious leaders, and friends who inspire others to climb higher and do more. Bodacious living is evident everywhere, but it's easy not to notice the remarkable people and happenings that are present all around.

With all its problems, society is making some healthy changes. Some folks are shifting their focus from material wealth to quality of life. Fathers have increased their involvement with their kids. Employees are turning down promotions and transfers so they can maintain a more consistent home life. Many parents are redirecting children from television to productive activities. More people of all ages are volunteering for community ventures, missionary trips, building projects, and to visit nursing facilities.

While organizing your final chapter, or recovering from a severe grief experience, explore using your talents to expand your horizons. Be a mentor; encourage others to live in ways that are satisfying and loving. Get involved with church activities, youth groups, and teaching Sunday school classes. Meaningful living is energizing and contagious. You can make a difference.

SAVORING THE WORLD

Savoring the world should be everyone's goal. It involves taking a bigger bite out of life, creating new possibilities, being venturesome and imaginative, and adding activities that enhance life and magnify happiness. That's living bodaciously. When you change, the world changes.

A seventy-five-year-old couple told me recently that they were planning a month-long trip to Paris to take French cooking lessons. Another senior couple held a family reunion for thirty-two people at a Holiday Inn to celebrate the new millennium. Their invitation read "Join us at the 'Cram-a-lot Inn.' Let's fill these four days with everything fun."

A local retiree decided to teach financial planning at the community college. Another retired couple attended the Stephen Ministry training course and became lay ministers at their church. Another group of church members meet at an elementary school once a week to tutor kids. Three neighborhood couples organized a monthly book study group. A newly retired teacher dedicated her first year of retirement to something she had always intended to do—reading the Bible, cover to cover. A fifty-year-old insurance salesman reads for the blind on weekends.

CREATIVE LIVING IS EVERYWHERE

To maximize life's adventures and free up your soul be open to new ideas and adventures. Forgive yourself and others—give up perfectionism and take steps in new directions. Engage in some outdoor activity, develop a new hobby, or enrich relationships. It doesn't take a major life change; simple things can get you started. For serious bird-watching, join a birding safari. Read *Alice in Wonderland, Charlotte's Web,* or *Tom Sawyer,* this time with adult eyes. Expand your sense of wonder, those transforming moments of elation. Watch a configuration of birds flying across the sky. Gaze at a sunset-painted sky with its magnificently changing beauty. Let cloud formations tickle your imagination. Listen to the rain. Enjoy watching a small child at play. Pause often to appreciate the pleasure of seeing, hearing, or feeling. Take pleasure in the detail of good art, the ability of music to transform the moment, the awareness of being totally alive. What opportunities surround you! Take time to say a prayer of thanksgiving for the blessings that are available in God's world.

Before falling asleep each night, think of something fun, pleasurable, or stimulating that you want to do the next day. Then do it—and delight in your accomplishment. Celebrations give zest to life, making you more aware of what you are achieving. Reward yourself for effort. Don't wait until every job is completed.

Live outside the lines. Dare to change. *You deserve to treat yourself better.*

it's never too late

When you look outward into your world, you can make some amazing discoveries, as Jenks and I did a few years ago. We joined an Elderhostel adventure to the Antarctic. Eighty-four seniors over sixty-five joined together for a journey most of us had only dreamed about. Our ship was a former Russian listening ship, designed to track foreign vessels. With a German crew, we sailed from the southern tip of South America in December, through the rough waters of the Drake Passage heading into the frozen Antarctic. At various stops in this mystical land, we left the ship and climbed into inflated rubber rafts that carried us almost to shore. Stepping off the rafts into water up to our knees, we waded to land. Our feet got cold even in wool socks and knee-high rubber boots. Thousands of penguins greeted us as we trudged up the snow-covered hills of the frozen continent. Some of us slid down the hills on our snowsuits. Sea lions and whales romped in the ocean around our ship, while an albatross with a ten-foot wingspan soared overhead. Starkly blue icebergs floated by with penguins and seals hitching a ride. Our journey was a bodacious adventure.[1]

You live in a wonderful time of discovery and progress. Keep in step by adjusting attitudes and making new choices. The art of living well is the challenge. Too often people put off doing things until it's too late . . . or they are shocked into action by some misfortune. Wake-up calls are events that can challenge you to pay attention to the way you are living, catapulting you to higher levels of exhilaration and bliss. You can make your life juicier. Awaken those dormant desires you have wanted to unleash. Seize opportunities that surround you. They are waiting for you to relish experiences of your choosing.

Look at all the life you have lived and survived. There has been a myriad of lessons that you've learned since you were born. The wonderment of walking, talking, tying your shoestrings. How to read and drive a car. That's a bunch of living and new beginnings. You are a miracle. A God original. Nobody else has lived a life like yours. It's too easy to take it all for granted and accept it without celebration.

STEPPING INTO THE FUTURE

Before recording ideas for future adventures, which will evolve into a plan, reenergize yourself by cleansing your past. Forgive yourself for mistakes. You did the best you could, most of the time. Nearly all decisions are based on partial information. If you knew back then what you know now, you might have made some different choices. For the same reasons most people who have wronged you were doing their best. Forgiving them will give you a sense of relief, and you'll enjoy a surge of freedom.

Don't waste energy dragging resentments, hurts, and disappointments into the future. The junkyards of life are overflowing with regrets about matters that can't be changed. Empty your garbage bag of grudges, and begin the rest of your life with a confident mind-set, a clean slate, and a wholesome spirit.

Now you are ready to anticipate stepping into your future. As your thoughts take you forward, write new goals in a journal. There is a magical factor in transferring thoughts from mind to paper. Record your mission statement—it is mind clearing to think about what you want to do with your life. Add adventures you want to experience. Include new ideas as you think of them. It's time to create a flexible blueprint for action—future memoirs worthy of you, a time to let your creative juices flow to satisfy and reward yourself. Be sure to include learning and loving. Of course you can't do everything and your ideas will change, but this is the beginning of where you intend to take yourself. Discuss your ideas and plans with family

213

and friends who will support and encourage you. Avoid sharing visions with those who have a knack for killing your enthusiasm.

Your future begins *now*. Reach a little further. Expand horizons. You can accomplish more than you ever imagined. Live abundantly. Add something special to your plans. Complete unfinished tasks. Are there words that need to be expressed or deeds to perform? People to see? Are there things you are doing that waste time and keep you from doing what you really enjoy?

Several years ago, my husband and I traveled to Oregon, Illinois, to visit relatives I had last seen sixty years before, when I was ten. Cousin Dick Little had stayed near his hometown, creating a dude ranch full of horses and family fun, while I had moved from one big city to another, nineteen times since my marriage. Together, Dick and I visited the old churchyard cemetery where our grandparents, Kate and John Little, are buried. We visited the farmhouse and cornfields that had been our playground when my family visited Uncle Ralph and Aunt Grace in 1933. Revisiting my heritage filled a lot of holes in my memory of childhood. It gave me a better sense of my ancestry and provided a wholesome connection to the past.

SPRINGBOARDS TO BODACIOUS LIVING

What's beckoning you into your new life that starts today? Have you resisted spending money or time on events that would create more rewarding experiences? Perhaps you have yearned to expand your knowledge of literature, gardening, or your family history. *Do it!* What about that shoebox of photos? Author Frances Weaver cleaned out her home but didn't know what to do with the zillion photographs. Some weren't even recognizable. She hit on a plan. Whenever she wrote letters, she included a picture or two. Didn't mention them, just enclosed them. Haystacks, the back end of a horse, the top of a baldheaded man, one hand on a car steering wheel, a family grouping with all their heads missing from the picture. Her photo box emptied. Others enjoyed the mystery. Wouldn't it be fun to know the reactions of all the people who received those special pictures?

A client told me she was taking tap dancing lessons. Something she had always wanted to do, but waited until she was fifty-five to start. Now she keeps her tap shoes in the trunk of her car, so she won't miss an opportunity to dance, if the occasion presents itself.

One couple hired a Spanish-speaking nanny and decided they could all benefit if the nanny taught Spanish to the whole family, while she learned English. The adventure was so satisfying that after several months, this couple chose to volunteer to teach an ESL (English as a second language) class in a Spanish-speaking church. Their passion became a family project.

Having the time of your life can be what's ahead for you. Fill your next chapters with the joy of redreaming. Dreams do come true. They are the beginning of accomplishing your goals. Create a bouquet from the blossoms you can reach. See humor in life. Lighten up; laugh at yourself. Don't let misunderstandings get in your way. While I was enjoying the country dance scene in the movie *The Horse Whisperer*, my husband leaned over and asked, "Do you want to go?" I was disappointed. I was enjoying the scene and did not want to leave. Turned out, he was asking if I wanted to go country dancing.

A young client, Taylor, had just turned thirty-seven. Her life would be ending soon, she told me, since her parents had died in their forties. She asked me how long I thought I'd live. My answer was, "I'm seventy-nine now, but I have lots of things to do before I die. So I see a big space, at least twenty-five years to fill."

"Well," she said, "you are older than my grandparents. I have a lot of projects, too. But I always felt I couldn't make long-range plans. Just live from day to day. Maybe I can plan to live longer than my parents. If you believe you have all that time ahead of you, I'm enlarging my future expectations, too." An intriguing—and intrigued—smile looked back at me.

Medical science and knowledge have increased life expectancy since your parents' time. Now science debunks a number of myths including the common belief that only genetics determine destiny. Researchers point out that lifestyle choices also become increasingly important in shaping the quality of later life. Are you including spirituality, prayer, and a connection with God in your plans? And the powerful determinants of good health, exercise, meaningful relationships, enjoyable activities, and healthy nutrition?

If you didn't "choose" parents with long-life genes, choose an upbeat attitude and a favorable lifestyle. Whatever time you have left, you can still make little pleasures count. The future is an unwritten chapter. You have the opportunity to design a masterpiece of worthwhile living. You are in charge of the road ahead. As Yogi Berra said, "When you come to a fork in the road, take it."

Song of Life

As I sit and ponder,
Just let my mind wander,

The tune of a song,
So meaningful and strong—
The song of my life
Filled with laughter and strife
Weaves its way through my head,
My mind slowly led
Back to things and times past,
Mem'ries that will last
'Til I'm old.
Precious jewels I must hold
Close to my heart,
For to make a fresh start,
In the world up above,
One must understand love.

—Kacie Jenkins, age 13, 1998

SPRINGBOARDS TO BODACIOUS LIVING

Activities that interest me:

_____

People I want to spend more time with:

_____

Some things I can do to improve relationships:

_____

Volunteer activities I will explore:

_____

Ways I want to increase my spirituality:

_____

Trips I want to take:

_____

Ways I could make myself more interesting, less irritating, and more lovable:

_____

Ways to improve the quality of my life:

_____

One dream I want to expand:

_____

Some things I want to let go of:

_____

Achievements I am going to celebrate:

_____

A list of things that will make my life more bodacious:

_____

One thing I will do this week to live with grace and gusto:

_____

17

SPIRITUALITY WHEN IT REALLY COUNTS

What if God had an answering machine and when you prayed you'd hear, "Thank you for calling heaven. Currently, we are busy helping other customers. Please listen to the following options: For requests, press 1. For thanksgiving, press 2. If you want to find out if a relative is here, press 3. For all other options, press 4. Our computers show you have already called twice today. Please hang up and give someone else a turn."

God's "phone system" is a mystery, and no one gets postcards from heaven saying, "Having a wonderful time. Wish you were here." Yet people believe in answered prayers, and an amazing number, from all cultures and religions, believe that their deceased loved ones still exist in an afterlife and, furthermore, that they will live with them on the other side of their own death. Even popular music reflects a belief in heaven with such titles as "I'm in Heaven," "Pennies from Heaven," and "Heaven Can Wait." Poems, literature, and movies paint many versions of the hereafter. Heaven is often defined as paradise, ultimate bliss, and "The Sweet By and By." The Bible tells us that heaven is a place with no pain or sorrow and that it is our true home.

Almost everyone believes *something* about heaven. Consequently, discussing your ideas about heaven with family and friends can make for very interesting conversation and a way to talk about your faith and your hopes for the future.

"I'm about to go dancing," were the delightful last words of one dying mother, who was denied the pleasure of dancing while on earth. She believed that heaven offered something amazing to look forward to. Fifteen-year-old Jeremy also told me his idea of heaven: "God always springs for the check. Everything is free." And April, age six, knew heaven had a floor, "Or else everybody would fall out. And it has windows where God pours out the rain."

FISH HEAVEN

Hanna's goldfish died. Two little, bright-eyed, ponytailed girls sat in my office talking about Fred, a Halloween gift from Aunt Nell. "He was fine when we left for school, but when we got home he was flopped over dead," Hanna explained.

Her five-year-old sister, Paige, sat cross-legged on the couch, tears trailing down her tanned cheeks. "Why did God let him die?" she cried. "He was a good fish. He'd smile at me when I fed him. Now he's dead. That's not fair."

Have you ever had similar thoughts about life and death and fairness?

Hanna and Paige shared their grief while I listened intently. Then I inquired, "Where did he get his name? Tell me what you remember about Fred. How was Fred buried?"

Eight-year-old Hanna moved to the edge of the couch. Her tears disappeared as she eagerly described the burial arrangements. "We wrapped Fred in a paper towel and laid him in a decorated shoebox. We paraded down our street with the shoebox, then we buried him in the backyard. First we ate orange Popsicles to honor him. Then everybody sang our church camp song, 'You Can't Get to Heaven on Roller Skates.' Now Fred is in fish heaven."

I asked, "Could you sing me the song you sang when you buried Fred?" They moved close together and sang.

> You can't get to heaven on roller skates,
> 'cause you'll roll right by them pearly gates.
> You can't get to heaven on roller skates,
> 'cause you'll roll right by them pearly gates.
> I ain't gonna grieve my Lord no more.
> I ain't gonna grieve my Lord no more,
> I ain't gonna grieve my Lord no more,
> I ain't gonna grieve my Lord no more.

We all clapped our hands while we joyfully sang several verses. I enjoyed singing along because I remembered the song from my own camp days.

Then Paige added, "Now Fred is up there swimming around with all his friends." She frowned and a puzzled expression came over her face. "How did Fred get to fish heaven from our backyard? That's a long swim."

While I contemplated the right answer, older and wiser Hanna came to my rescue.

"Well, Paige, first you need to know there is no such place as fish heaven. We just say that. There is just one big heaven that covers the whole wide earth, and everybody goes there. Unless they're really bad. Gramma and Grampa are there. Uncle Dan, who died of cancer, is there. Nobody knows how Fred got to heaven, but it doesn't matter. It just happens, and that's all we need to know."

Paige chimed in, "If you leave bubblegum under the table you won't go to heaven. But we know heaven is a happy place where there are lots of flowers and rainbows. And if you want to build a snowman, you can always find enough snow."

Hanna explained, "And little girls get turned into angels. God does the best he can with the boys."

Paige hinted, "And everybody likes you, and nobody pushes you down. You don't have to get shots or go to the hospital. Nobody cries and everybody's happy."

The idea of an afterlife is so pervasive in our culture that even young children have ideas about heaven and an afterlife—some good ones, don't you think . . . even if not entirely "theologically correct"?

SPIRITUALITY

What do you believe about the hereafter? Some people think they will go to heaven if they are good, but as a Christian, I believe that it is faith in Christ that gets people into heaven, not "being good." A saintly friend told me, "I'm afraid my sins will prevent me from entering the pearly gates. I have failed to live up to God's expectations of me." My husband, knowing heaven comes to us from God's grace and not our earthly works, told this loving ninety-two-year-old widow, "Eloise, the trumpets will be blaring to celebrate your arrival in heaven." I don't believe God keeps score. And you don't have to pass your "finals" to be welcomed into heaven. God forgives you when you accept Christ, and heaven is a place where you will be unconditionally loved.

But for others, the belief in heaven, much less salvation, is part of a spiritual journey they haven't yet made. Julie, whose seven-year-old-daughter, Kimberly, had leukemia, found that it was an impossible trip. She wished she could believe in God and a hereafter. "That would be consoling, but it sounds like make-believe to me." Julie and her husband were scientists, and believing in anything "unknown" didn't make sense to them. Then she asked, "How do you develop faith in a God? I'm jealous of people who have a sense of spirituality. I don't know how to get there."

While talking with Julie, I wished I had a greater knowledge and understanding on the subject of faith and salvation and heaven, and I prayed God would speak through me to answer this sad woman's searching. I am saddened by those whose faith is limited to "proven" truths, when many of those "facts" continue to shift. Science is not as "absolute" as some people insist. Many changes occur as explorations result in new breakthroughs. My grandson's college biology teacher explained how we used to believe certain truths, and now we have more up-to-date information, so the "truth" has changed. Having faith in only what has been proven is getting harder and harder.

God, however, does not change, and your faith in Him and His Son assures you of a future here—and in the hereafter. When there is no faith in God, there is no hope for the future. I believe that faith—your spiritual growth—begins with love. Jesus tells us to "love the Lord your God with all your heart and with all your soul and with all your mind. This is the first and greatest command-ment. And the second is like it: 'Love your neighbor as yourself'" (Matthew 22:37–38). In many ways, when people show love, they are responding to God's power to open their hearts to Him and to others. For instance, teaching children to forgive, to show apprecia-tion for life, and to trust are all evidence of spirituality—a belief in God's love and unchanging nature.

I don't believe, however, that you have to create an elaborate plan in order to open your mind and heart to spiritual growth. Being still and letting God in happens when you allow it. Prayer, meditation, poems, music, and special writings can provide a context in which your spirit can grow and endure. Persevering in the journey, and connecting to God enables you to view life and death from a more comforting perspective. Belief in an afterlife provides a type of hope, and expressing hope is a prayer that is an important vehicle for the human spirit to find meaning. Faith transcends grief, pain, and loss.

I reminded Julie that God is not lost. He doesn't need finding. Even when people see themselves as being far from God, He is never far from them. He longs for a relationship with us and He welcomes us with open arms and the bountiful promises of heaven. I assured Julie that she was more spiritual than she realized. Her search for answers and her love for Kimberly were evidence of that. God will find her. With all the worry and concern she had for her sick little girl, her anger and resistance to God were understandable—a normal and natural reaction to her grief.

So was her hunger for more spirituality. All of us, including those who insist on believing in only what can be seen or touched, will sooner or later find ourselves struggling with a need for something more. Science, at its best, provides limited information about how things work, but it can't go beyond its own limitations. Nor does it offer comfort or a cure for grief. Faith is relying on the infinite power of God to graciously and wisely see you through all that you understand and all that you don't understand . . . in life, in death, and in the life to come.

There are many things I don't understand about the nature of life and death; it is truly God's mystery. Believing that God is in charge of the world and all that is in it may take a leap of faith, but Mom and Dad gave me the gift of trusting in a loving God. I learned to believe that I was loved by my parents and my God. In turn, as my parents got older they trusted me to love and care for them. When Dad decided to live out his final years at a nursing home, he asked us to clean out his house and take his things home to Houston. Everything came to Texas and was stored in our garage while our cars sat out in the sweltering heat. I felt over-whelmed looking at all the stuff we hauled home. I didn't know where to start or what to do. I would walk into the garage, sit, and look at all the belongings I had grown up with, and memories would come rushing back. I touched the smooth cherry desk, felt the leather covers on the old, old books. I opened one box and discovered all of Mom's kitchen utensils—the flour sifter, the wooden spoons, and the pancake turner—and tears rolled down my cheeks. I felt immobilized and guilty not only because I had all of these personal items but because of the *reason* I had them.

Weeks went by, and our cars were still parked in the driveway. I had trouble sleeping. I felt a tightness in my chest, a loneliness in my heart. What should I do with these cherished possessions? How should I go about making the right decisions regarding them and honoring my parents?

Several months went by, then one night I had a dream. My mother, with her lovely silver hair, rosy cheeks, and soft brown eyes sat at my breakfast table. She was wearing a lavender housedress I had given her many years before. We sipped tea from some of her English bone china cups, the ones with tiny pink roses around the edge. Mom reached across the table and held my hands in hers. I felt the softness in her touch.

She spoke in her loving voice that had cradled me through the years. "Margie, you have been such a joy and satisfaction. Your sensitive spirit has uplifted me since you were a child. Your laugh-ter has filled my heart. You have blessed me in more ways than I can ever tell you. God was good when He sent you to me when I was really too old to deal with a baby. You have always been special to me. Now it is time for you to bring my things into your home. They belong here. Polish them up and treasure them as I did. I will always be with you."

I woke up with a jolt.

Somehow, seeing my mother in that dream and hearing her voice gave me permission to incorporate her lovely and cherished possessions into my home. I had never before had such an emotional dream experience. It was beautiful.

Some might say I was just looking for an excuse to rid myself of guilt. Others might suggest that I put meaning into the dream that was not there, but I believe my mother came to me in that dream. I felt her spirit with me at the kitchen table. I don't understand it, but the mystery warms my soul. Insight and understanding usually come in surprising ways. For me, that dream was God's way of reassuring me of Mom's presence even in death.

Heaven is like that: a mystery that is beyond my understanding. I know that God is good and wants the best for all of us. He is eternal, and He will always be our guide, if we are willing to follow and trust Him. He promises us a heaven where all our questions will be answered, where we will be free of pain, and where we will be joined with other believers in love and happiness. I believe that heaven will be so glorious that we cannot even imagine the peace and joy that is in store for us. A grand reunion awaits me when Mom and Dad and my God welcome me with open arms into my life after death.

Colors of the Sunset

Moon a shadow—
Colors glisten
Rainbow shimmers through the sky

Sun, a painter
Settles lower
Mountains tell her,
"Don't be shy"

Blue and Purple
Dance together
Turning circles in the air

Green and Yellow
Softly whisper
Secrets only they can share

Red and Orange
Tell a story
I can hear them laugh and cry

Pink and Violet
Smile in wonder—
"What a view from up so high!"

—BRODIE JENKINS, my ten-year-old granddaughter
November 1998

RECOMMENDED RESOURCES

Albom, Mitch. *Tuesdays with Morrie.* New York: Doubleday, 1997.
A college professor shares his experience of dying and provides profound wisdom and insight.

Buckman, Robert. *I Don't Know What to Say.* Toronto: Key Porter Books, Limited, 1988.
Written for family and friends of a dying person. Gives actual words to say and techniques for listening to someone who is dying

Byock, Ira, M.D. *Dying Well: The Prospect for Growth at the End of Life.* New York: Riverhead Books, 1997.
Sounds both a note of hope and a call to action as he shows that there is a better way for the medical profession to care for the dying. Focuses on hospice care and services.

Callanan, Maggie, and Patricia Kelley. *Final Gifts.* New York: Bantam Books, 1993.
Hospice nurses who have tended the terminally ill share their intimate experiences with patients at the edge of life.

de Hennezel, Marie. *Intimate Death*. New York: Alfred A. Knopf, 1997.
How the dying can teach us how to live.

Fulghum, Robert. *From Beginning to End: Rituals of Our Lives*. New York: Villard Books, a division of Random House, 1995.
Explores the public, private, and secret rituals that mark the passage of human life—births, anniversaries, and funerals.

Heatherley, Joyce Landorf. *The Inheritance*. Salado, Tex.: Balcony Publishing, 1989.
Beautifully written by a uniquely gifted Christian communicator who is able to convey compassion, humor, and gentle conviction, reminding us that our inheritance includes much more than "things."

Heatherley, Joyce Landorf. *Mourning Song*. Salado, Tex.:, Balcony Publishing, 1994.
Answers to pain-filled questions: "Why do I have to die?" and "Why does my loved one have to die?"

Kubler-Ross, Elisabeth. *On Death and Dying*. New York: Macmillan Publishing Co. Inc., 1969.
This book brought death out of the darkness and offers insight and understanding so that all those who have contact with the terminally ill can do more to help them.

Kushner, Harold. *When Bad Things Happen to Good People*. New York: Avon Books, 1983.
This book brings comfort for times when bad things happen.

Morris, Virginia. *Talking about Death Won't Kill You.* New York: Workman, 2002.
Personal tales and practical details to empower the living and the dying.

Neeld, Elizabeth Harper. *Seven Choices.* New York: Clarkson J. Potter, Inc., 1990.
Taking steps to a new life after losing someone you love.

Nuland, Sherwin B. *How We Die.* New York: Vintage Books, a division of Random House, Inc., 1993.
A distinguished surgeon describes the mechanisms of cancer, heart attack, stroke, AIDS, and Alzheimer's disease with clinical exactness and poetic eloquence and sensitivity, restoring death to its ancient place in human existence.

Remen, Rachel Naomi. *Kitchen Table Wisdom.* New York: Riverhead Books, 1996.
A pioneer in medicine of the future, Remen shows how physicians can become healers by being alchemists of the soul.

Schultz, Susan Polis, ed. *Creeds to Live By, Dreams to Follow.* Boulder, Col.: Blue Mountain Press, 1987.
A delightful book of poems and pictures that delight the soul.

Shedd, Charlie, and Martha Shedd. *Grandparents Family Book.* Garden City, N.Y.: Doubleday and Co., 1982.
A well-known minister and author of forty books, along with his wife, Martha, designed this book to help grandparents write the most interesting biography a grandchild will

ever read. A blessed connection between generations, looking backward and into the future with Christian guidance to record a timeless record for your family.

Shotwell, Barbara, and Nancy Randolph Greenway. *Pass It On.* New York: Hyperion, 2000.
A practical approach to the fears and facts of planning your estate.

Shriver, Maria. *What's Heaven.* New York: St. Martins Press, 1999.
Death eventually touches every family and this treasure of a book—for people of all faiths—is a starting point for parents who must talk about this difficult topic with their children.

Voist, Judith. *Necessary Losses.* New York: Ballantine Books, 1985.
Information about effects of grief and loss throughout life.

Westberg, Granger. *Good Grief.* Philadelphia: Fortress Press, 1962.
Seeing the value of grief and accepting its realities.

The Funeral Consumers Alliance can be reached at 1-800-765-0107. Other information can also be found on their web Site:www.funerals.org.

NOTES

CHAPTER 9

1. Lisa Carlson, *Caring for the Dead.* (Hinesburg, Vt,: Upper Access, Inc., 1998).

CHAPTER 10

1. Nicholas A. Christakis and Elizabeth B. Lamont, "Extent and Determinants of Error in Doctors' Prognoses in Terminally Ill Patients: Prospective Cohort Study," *British Medical Journal* 320 (19 February 2000): 469–473. Quoted on-line in "Doctors Overestimate Survival Times, Dying Patients Lose Choice and Fulfillment of Plans," *PSA Rising* (http://www.psa-rising.com/medicalpike/hospicelate-chicfeb00.htm).

CHAPTER 12

1. Ira Byock, M.D. *Dying Well: The Prospect for Growth at the End of Life* (New York: Riverhead Books, 1997).

CHAPTER 15

1. Author's note: Psychiatrist Elisabeth Kubler-Ross, in her landmark, best-selling book, *On Death and Dying* (New York: Macmillan Publishing Co., Inc., 1969), lists five stages of grief: Denial and Isolation, Anger, Bargaining, Depression, and Acceptance. Dr. Edwin Shneidman, who works extensively with the dying, wrote *Voices of Death* (New York: Kodansha America, Inc., 1995) and names other emotional states: Stoicism, Rage, Guilt, Terror, Fear, Surrender, Heroism, Dependency, Need for Control, and Fight for Autonomy and Dignity.

CHAPTER 16

1. Elderhostel programs provide thousands of adventures to seniors looking for a chance to explore new places and learn from lectures. They can be contacted at www.elderhostel.org or 1-877-426-8056.

INDEX